Networking:

How To Enrich Your Life and Get Things Done

Donald R. Woods
Shirley D. Ormerod

Pfeiffer
& COMPANY

Amsterdam • Johannesburg • London
San Diego • Sydney • Toronto

Copyright © 1993 by Pfeiffer & Company
ISBN 0-88390-363-6
Library of Congress Catalog Card Number 92-47413

Library of Congress Cataloging-in-Publication Data
Woods, Donald R.
    Networking: how to enrich your life and get things done / Donald
R. Woods and Shirley D. Ormerod.
      p.   cm.
    Includes bibliographical references.
    ISBN 0-88390-363-6
    1. Social networks—United States—Handbooks, manuals, etc.
I. Ormerod, Shirley D.   II. Title.
HM131.W62   1993
302—dc20

92-47413
CIP

Pfeiffer & Company
International Publishers
8517 Production Avenue
San Diego, California 92121-2280
USA
(619) 578-5900; FAX (619) 578-2042

This book is printed on acid-free, recycled stock
that meets or exceeds the minimum GPO
and EPA specifications for recycled paper.

PREFACE

Networking is probably the most important skill you can possess. It enriches your day-to-day life and enables you to get things done effectively and efficiently. Current business literature has much to say about networking, suggesting that it is an essential skill for leaders and for anyone who must cope with continually changing technology. In addition, the literature on life skills recommends drawing on a network for support in times of crisis. Yet despite how often the terms "network" and "networking" appear, few guidelines are available on the process of networking.

This book is a unique synthesis of our own experiences and those of people we interviewed and observed. It presents a way to enrich your life and to get things done through networking. Few "how-to" books have been written on the role of networking either in enriching one's life or in getting things done, and to our knowledge none have been written on how to apply networking to do both. Our book evolved from a series of workshops that we developed for students in the Engineering and Management Program at McMaster University in Hamilton, Ontario, Canada, and that have been conducted for various organizations, agencies, and industries. The ideas and activities included here have been tested in those workshops.

In this book we do not try to teach you how to network by telling you success and failure stories. Instead, we offer you a chance to empower yourself to network by practicing the necessary skills. You are asked to complete activities, not simply to read passively; included are forty-eight activities that will develop your ability to set and reach personal goals through networking.

By reading this book, you will learn your networking strengths and how to reinforce those strengths in your future efforts. You will also uncover areas in which you wish to improve, and you will begin a process of developing the awareness and skills you need to effect that improvement. Regardless of your present level of skill at networking, there is something in this book for you.

You may choose to work through the book on your own; if you do, the materials are complete and you need no additional resources. However, some people benefit from discussing their ideas and testing their assumptions with others. If you are one of those people, you may want to work through this book with a partner or in a group. Trainers may wish to use this book or selections from it for a two-hour, half-day, one-day, or two-day workshop.

Also, although we see the components of this book as combining to form a comprehensive whole, we have designed the individual chapters so that they can essentially stand alone. In this way you can focus on an individual topic, such as nurturing your network or expanding your network.

We acknowledge and thank the many workshop participants who gave us feedback and suggestions about our networking materials and activities. Special thanks go to Marnie Spears, John Medcof, and Suzanne Kresta, all of McMaster University; to Joan Balinson, Ted McMeekin, and Diane E. Woods; and to our colleagues at work and in the community, who provided insight through their examples. Our special thanks also go to Carol Nolde for her valued input and professional contributions to our book.

Donald R. Woods
Shirley D. Ormerod

Hamilton, Ontario, Canada
January, 1993

Contents

1

Networks and Networking

OVERVIEW OF THIS CHAPTER

In this chapter you will learn definitions of "network" and "networking," the characteristics of each, and why networking is a vital skill that everyone needs to develop. You will also be introduced to the process of "bridging" from one network to another.

WHAT IS A NETWORK?

Your network consists of *all the people you know*. It includes people you do and do not enjoy, people from all walks of life, people you know extremely well, and those with whom you are only acquainted. Frequently people underestimate the size of their networks. Consider that your network may include all of these groups and possibly many others:

- Your relatives;
- Your co-workers;
- Your friends and social acquaintances;
- Your fellow students in your high school graduating class;
- The members of the church, the professional organizations, or the clubs that you belong to;
- People you have met on vacations or during workshops;
- The season ticket holders who sit beside you at your local stadium; and
- All the service people in your life: doctors, dentists, mechanics, plumbers, postal workers, delivery people, and so on.

It may surprise you to learn that the average network consists of 1,000 to 2,500 people. Figure 1 is an illustration of one person's network, shown in a spider-web configuration. Each dot represents one member of the network, and members are organized according to categories. The circles that radiate from the center of the spider web represent degrees of intimacy and dependability: the closer the circle is to the center, the greater the degree of intimacy or dependability in the relationship.

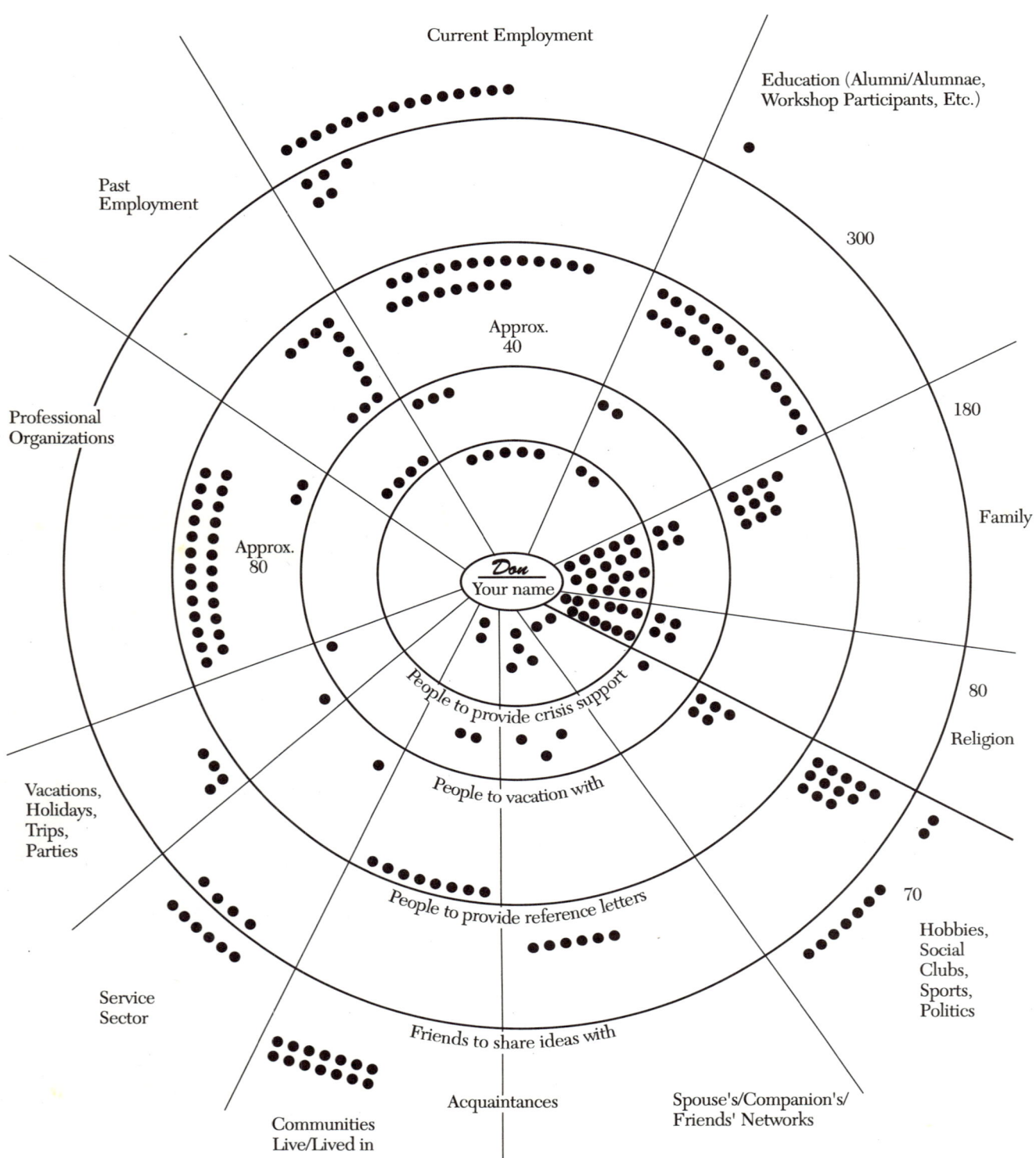

Current Employment

Education (Alumni/Alumnae, Workshop Participants, Etc.)

Past Employment

300

Professional Organizations

Approx. 40

180

Family

Approx. 80

Don
Your name

80

People to provide crisis support

Religion

People to vacation with

Vacations, Holidays, Trips, Parties

People to provide reference letters

70

Service Sector

Hobbies, Social Clubs, Sports, Politics

Friends to share ideas with

Communities Live/Lived in

Acquaintances

Spouse's/Companion's/ Friends' Networks

Figure 1. An Illustration of a Network

Your network is:

- Larger than you might think;

- Suited to your own wants and needs;

- Alive, expanding and contracting with your changing life circumstances;

- The result of your decisions to maintain particular levels of intimacy or distance with certain people;

- Related to your goals, your support system, and your access to power and influence to get things done; and

- Connected to the networks of others.

The last characteristic of your network, that it is connected to the networks of others, means that you can "bridge" from the people you know to the people that others know. Thus, you can bridge from one network to another and another and so on until you make contact with a "target" person. This process of *bridging networks* can give you access to people whom you might have previously considered to be inaccessible.

Activity 1. Bridging

Think of someone you never thought you could meet: Mother Teresa, Mikhail Gorbachev, Desmond Tutu, or some other famous person. First imagine the people who might be in that person's network. Then identify the people in your network who might provide potential leads. Think of various paths of contacts that might help you meet your goal.

WHAT IS NETWORKING?

People's needs are the basis of networking. Consider these examples:

Dave announces to Margaret as he storms out of the house, "I want a divorce!" Shocked and bewildered, Margaret wonders how she is going to respond to her husband's announcement.

Suzette has just seen twenty-three years with her employer go down the drain. She was fired today and does not know what to do next.

Franz has been assigned the task of ensuring that his company's move to its new headquarters goes smoothly. He has completed similar tasks before, but not one so large and so much in the spotlight. He is unsure about how to proceed.

Maria has a terrific idea about how her company can save money by changing the way that it handles invoices, but she does not know how to convert her idea into reality.

Ian feels that it is time to break away from his employer, the Chartered Accountant Company, and set up his own business as a financial analyst. He wonders how to determine whether he will have enough business.

Ruby has painted a "masterpiece" and wants to share her excitement and sense of accomplishment with someone. But whom?

All of these people have needs—the need for a listener, the need for someone with whom to share joys and sorrows, the need for information and help in getting a job done, and the need to find new opportunities when current ones disappear or cease to be fulfilling. People's needs change from day to day and from year to year. Whatever those needs are, they usually are satisfied through or with the aid of others. The process of satisfying needs through others—of interacting with people in order to enrich your life and to get things done—is referred to as *networking*.

Enriching Our Lives

Networking is more than sharing information or using people to reach a goal (for example, finding a job). It involves giving as well as taking; therefore, the motivation to network should be not only self-interest but also a genuine interest in others. In fact, the authors' perception is that networking is about five times more *giving* than *taking*.

As givers we listen; provide information, advice, contacts, and emotional support; encourage; empathize; and help. Everyone wants a life filled with a sense of achievement and self-worth, of happiness balanced with challenge and opportunity. Everyone needs others to help cope with the "lowlights" of life and to share the highlights. The process of reaching out to others and sharing with them provides the richness and warmth of living. Think, for instance, of the inner joy you feel when you have helped someone.

A rich life is not gained exclusively by giving to a network, though. When we draw on our networks, we ask for and receive information, emotional support, encouragement, empathy, and help. The people who compose a network help in surviving crises; they give the "warm fuzzies" of life. A network provides almost unlimited and unexpected riches to help a person through the tough times. Here is an example:

Jane's friend, Jeremy, was asked to retire early from a major manufacturing company that had just been through several years of transition to total quality management (TQM). Now Jeremy, who has a lot of hands-on experience, is struggling to set up his own company to help businesses implement TQM. Harold, another of Jane's friends, is the president of a company that conducts courses on TQM. However, the personnel in Harold's company lack the hands-on experience that Jeremy has. With Jeremy's permission, Jane told Harold about Jeremy and suggested that both men might benefit by chatting with each other. By bringing the two together, Jane gave to her network. In return she received the pleasure that comes from trying to help friends.

Getting Things Done

Networking not only enriches our lives; it also helps us to get things done. Using networking to get things done has two advantages over other approaches:

1. *People offer the best help.* People—not books, television, newspapers, or magazines—are the most accessible and pertinent source of information for almost any problem. For example, if your bathroom faucet is leaking, would you prefer reading a book on how to repair a faucet, watching a video on the subject, or enlisting the help of a friend who has successfully repaired faucets?

2. *Rarely can one person get things done on his or her own.* Everyone needs help from others. Another person may supply an extra pair of hands, duplicate a report, provide money to support an idea, or give feedback about an idea. The help that others provide can offer insight into many areas:

- How to perceive or approach the environment (at work, at home, and in social circumstances);
- How to identify opportunities and problems;
- How to implement ideas;
- How to convince others to "buy in" to a particular point of view or project;
- Who would be effective on teams or committees;
- How to reach personal goals; and
- How to obtain access to others.

CHARACTERISTICS OF EFFECTIVE NETWORKING

Effective networking[1] is:

1. Being self-confident, loving yourself enough to love and give to others;
2. Honoring the fundamental rights of all people to be respected, to have needs and feelings, to decide, and to have opinions;
3. Giving—without expectations about what you might get in return (anticipate giving five times what you think you might ever get);

---

[1] These characteristics are based on Boe and Youngs (1989) and the authors' experience. The authors refer to the first seven characteristics as "the five basic skills and the two fundamentals of networking." The details of these skills and fundamentals are explored in Chapters 3 and 4.

4. Being able to say "thank you," "I'm wrong," and "I'm sorry";
5. Caring enough to do and be your very best, to excel at what you do;
6. Developing trust and warmth with others and treating others as equals;
7. Knowing and being known by many, being visible, and knowing quality details about others;
8. Understanding that maintaining the network takes time and hard work;
9. Being organized, systematic, and prepared;
10. Being positive and making the most of opportunities when they arise;
11. Recognizing the "down" side of networking (primarily having to say "no");
12. Having goals and working to achieve them; and
13. Unabashedly drawing on your network for ideas and support in enriching your life and in getting things done.

WHY NETWORKS AND EFFECTIVE NETWORKING ARE VITAL

For the following reasons, networking is an important skill that everyone can benefit from developing:

1. Networking provides support and encouragement for the joys, frustrations, and tragedies of life.
2. People are the most valuable source of information and help in achieving goals, gaining support and influence, providing access, and getting things done.
3. Most people network intuitively without understanding how or why they network. Sometimes they unwittingly violate some of the skills and fundamentals of networking. By increasing awareness of these skills and fundamentals, everyone can improve.
4. Some people do not know how to network.
5. Some people exercise only the "taking" function of networking and omit the "giving," without realizing the damage they are doing.
6. Many people practice networking as a way to get things done effectively and efficiently but omit the other, equally important dimension of networking: to have a richer life.

Skill at networking can be improved dramatically by reflecting on the process and by completing activities designed to foster improvement. This book was written to meet the needs of those who wish to improve their abilities to network effectively.

THIS BOOK AND WHAT YOU WILL GAIN FROM IT

The subsequent chapters in this book are relatively independent. Here is a brief summary of the topics they cover:

- *Chapter 2:* Setting goals for networking;

- *Chapters 3 and 4:* The five basic skills and the two fundamentals of networking;

- *Chapter 5:* Nurturing your network;

- *Chapter 6:* Expanding your network;

- *Chapter 7:* The "down" side of networking;

- *Chapter 8:* Using your network as a resource;

- *Chapter 9:* Fostering networking in an organization; and

- *Chapter 10:* Planning how to improve your networking.

There are two kinds of activities in this book, ones intended to start you thinking about various aspects of networking and ones that ask you to write down your ideas. The thought provokers, which involve no written composition, are presented in shaded boxes, whereas the activities that do involve written composition are designated with an illustration of a hand holding a pencil. The thought provokers are optional. However, completing the activities that involve writing is recommended if you are to develop an understanding of your network and how to use it effectively.

After you have completed this book, you will have developed an awareness of:

- The characteristics of networks;

- The skills and fundamentals of networking;

- The required attitude toward networking—a genuine interest in others;

- Your current network (its members and their relationships to you);

- The strengths of your network and areas in which you would like to improve your network;

- The people you might want to bring into your network;

- The ways in which you might use bridging to achieve goals;

- The fundamental human rights and the guidelines for "interpersonal Shangri-la"; and

- Covey's (1989) model of developing trust and the implications of this model.

As a result of working through the material in this book, you will be able to do the following things:

- Apply criteria to set personal goals for your network;
- Generate practical ideas and suggestions for giving to your network;
- Think of ways to nurture, expand, and use your network;
- Understand the negative aspects of networking and devise ways to cope with them;
- Draw on your network in a crisis;
- Identify the current "corporate/institutional culture" at your workplace;
- Get others to "buy in" to your ideas;
- Understand and use the stages of the change process;
- Generate ways to create positive environments that recognize the importance of networking and encourage effective networking; and
- Create an action plan to implement ideas from this book.

Activity 2. Current Awareness and Skill

Perceiving your own personal growth is challenging. One way to gauge your progress is to reflect on your networking awareness and skill before you read further and then to reassess your awareness and skill after you have completed this book.

How *aware* are you of your current network and of what you do when you are networking? On the following continuum, circle the number that describes your level of awareness.

0   1   2   3   (4)   5   6   7   8   9   10

Unaware; I just do it	Somewhat aware	Very aware; I can describe details

How *skilled* are you at networking? On the following continuum, circle the number that describes your level of skill.

0   (1)   2   3   4   5   6   7   8   9   10

Poor	Fair	Good	Very good	Excellent

SUMMARY

Your network is defined as "all the people you know." It is large, personal, alive, the result of personal decisions, related to your goals, and connected to the networks of others. You have people in your network from different sectors of your life, and you know people at different levels of intimacy.

"Bridging" is a process whereby you can have access to a person you do not know by contacting members of your network, who then contact members of their own networks, and so on until the "target" person is reached. With patience and skill, you can have access to anyone in the world.

Networking is "interacting with people in your network in order to have a rich life and to get things done." It is based on particular attitudes, skills, and principles; it involves setting goals, giving to the network, and using the network as a resource. The primary "down" side of networking is that sometimes you have to say "no."

Whether you are skilled or unskilled, your effectiveness can be improved by reflecting on your current network and on why and how you go about the process of networking.

─────────────── ╫╫╫ ───────────────

✎ *Activity 3. Discoveries from Chapter 1*

In the following columns, write what you have discovered from reading and working through this chapter. Please take the time to do the writing now. Such writing is important in helping you to consolidate what you are learning about yourself and about networking. Also add how you might apply the discovered ideas in your daily living.

Discovery

Applications

Definition of "network" and its characteristics

Larger than I thought. More than just close friends.

Definition of "networking" and its characteristics

Start with loving myself. Then loving & respecting others. Constantly nurturing the parts of the network. Much more giving than taking.

Discovery	Applications
Bridging	
Why networks and networking are vital	
Other	

┤┼┤

✍ *Activity 4. Action Plan for the Coming Week*

Choose one of your discoveries and apply the implications during the coming week. (For example, if you discovered that networking involves more giving than taking, a possible application might be to spend some time in the next week acknowledging your gratitude to the people in your network with a face-to-face thank-you, a personal note, or a phone call.) Write down your plan of action in the space that follows.

2

Setting Goals for Networks and Networking

OVERVIEW OF THIS CHAPTER

Networks and networking should be related to your goals and should help you to achieve your goals. In this chapter you will identify some long- and short-term goals and determine whether your current network and networking skills are helping or hindering you in achieving those goals. Criteria are suggested to help you decide and take appropriate action.

YOUR PERSONAL GOALS

The importance of goal setting has been stressed by a number of people. For example, Locke, Shaw, Saari, and Latham (1981) suggest that we all work more effectively and efficiently if we have goals. Similarly, Morrison, White, and van Velson (1987, p. 172) state that one of the five commandments for success is to "Know what you want out of life!" And Covey (1989) sees goal setting as being one of the seven habits of effective people.

But how do you devise a goal? Here are some things to remember when creating goals for yourself:

1. *A good goal is written.* Until you commit a goal to writing, it remains elusive, changeable, and vague. Try not to worry about whether your first writing effort results in a polished statement. Here is an example of a first effort at writing a goal: "Get to know people with marketing experience."

2. *A good goal is broken down into milestones.* Many of your goals will take a long time to achieve. Consequently, you need to break each big goal into small steps that can be achieved along the way. These small steps become milestones of progress that let you know you are headed in the right direction and that offer you a psychological boost and encourage you to keep going. Remember that being positive and optimistic is important.

3. *A good goal includes criteria.* Criteria are measures of achievement. For example, for the goal cited earlier—"get to know people with marketing experience"—one criterion might be "with each of three people, spend at least three hours

talking informally about anything and one hour discussing marketing." Another criterion might be "each of the three people should have at least four years of direct market experience." As you add criteria to your goal, two things will become clearer: (1) what you need to do and (2) how you will know when you have achieved your goal. Criteria are often challenging to create but necessary. Persevere!

4. *A good goal is consistent with your lifetime objectives.* Your lifetime objectives, goals, any subgoals, and milestones should all be consistent. One way to check whether a specific goal fits with your lifetime objectives is to ask why you want to achieve that goal. If you discover inconsistency, then you must rework the goal or your lifetime objectives or both.

5. *A good goal is achievable.* Working toward any goal means that you must dedicate resources to that end. You need to determine what resources are needed and ensure that you have those resources and any necessary support. If you do not have—and cannot get—the essential resources and support, the goal is not achievable and should be abandoned.

———————————— ┼┼┼ ————————————

✐ *Activity 5. Goal Setting*

In the space provided, write out one goal you would like to achieve in the next five or ten years.

If you have trouble identifying a goal, try using the following ideas to trigger your inner feelings:

- "If you knew that you were going to be struck dead by lightning in six months, how would you live until then?" (Lakein, 1973, p. 30)

- If you received a telegram tonight that made you feel ecstatic, what would it say? (If it states that you won money, explain how you would spend your money.)

- If you had one wish, what would it be?

- If the following people wrote your eulogy after you died, what would each of them say about you: family member? friend? colleague from work? person from a community organization to which you belonged? (Covey, 1989)

After you have come up with your ten-year or five-year goal, create one-year and six-month milestones for your goal. Also identify criteria and needed support.

Ten-year goal: **Criteria**

Support that I need:

Five-year goal: **Criteria**

Support that I need:

One-year milestone: **Criteria**

Support that I need:

Six-month milestone: **Criteria**

Support that I need:

YOUR CURRENT NETWORK

As you learned in Chapter 1, your network consists of many people, probably many more than you might have imagined. You are associated with these people in varying degrees of intimacy and to varying degrees of dependence. The contexts in which you know people are as follows:

- Your family, in-laws, relatives;

- People you went to school with (grammar or public school, high school, college or university, workshops or seminars or other short courses);

- People from work, both at previous places of employment and at your current workplace;

- People who share your religious affiliation;

- People who belong to your social clubs, people who share your hobbies, people with whom you do volunteer work, people with whom you play sports or watch sports, people who have season tickets for the same events that you regularly attend (the theater, the opera, and so on);

- People who belong to the same organizations, agencies, and societies that you do (members of the Rotary, the Chamber of Commerce, the Big Sisters, United Appeal, Red Cross, and so on);

- People in your current neighborhood and in neighborhoods where you used to live, people you have met while on vacation or holiday, people of the same nationality, people of the same ethnic background or culture;

- People you have met at spontaneous events (at parties, at restaurants, and so on);

- People you know through the experiences and interests of those who are so close to you (your spouse, companion or significant other, confidant) that you feel you are an intimate part of their networks;

- People who provide services for you: doctors, dentists, lawyers, repair person-nel, service-station operators, bankers, clerks, storekeepers, paper and mail carriers, and so on;

- People you can count on for crisis support (if you are fired from your job, bereaved, divorced, wiped out by a fire, convicted of a crime, diagnosed with a terminal disease, or bankrupted);

- People you would vacation or holiday with for two weeks (people who accept you "warts and all"; who confide in you and whom you confide in; with whom you can openly share your joys and sorrows, your successes and failures);

- People who know you well enough to write a reference letter for you about your personal character or your professional competence;

- Friends/acquaintances whose names and professions you know and who know you to the same extent; and

- People you recognize and know of, but they do not know you (the president of a professional association or of the company).

— ┼┼┼ —

✍ Activity 6. Networking Table

Completing the following table will help you come up with information to use in the next activity, creating a spider-web diagram of your network. On the far left of the table are the contexts just discussed. In Column 1 write down the names of schools that you have attended, companies that you have worked for, professional organizations that you are or have been affiliated with, communities that you have lived in, past and present hobbies, and religion (for example, the names of churches or synagogues that you have attended). In Column 2 write the names or initials of people who first come to mind in each of the contexts. Consider starting with your résumé or your list of people to whom you send cards or greetings for special occasions (birthdays, Christmas, Hanukkah, and so on). In Column 3 list the names or initials of the next ten people you think of. Finally, complete Column 4 with the estimated total in each context.

	Column 1 *Institutions*	Column 2 *First people who come to mind*	Column 3 *Next ten who come to mind*	Column 4 *Estimated total*
Family				
Education				
Employment				

	Column 1 *Institutions*	**Column 2** *First people* *who come* *to mind*	**Column 3** *Next ten who* *come to mind*	**Column 4** *Estimated total*
Professional Organizations				
Spontaneous Events				
Service Sector				
Communities				
Spouse's/ Companion's/ Friends' Networks				
Hobbies				
Religion				

———————————— ┼┼┼ ————————————

✍ Activity 7. Diagram of Your Network

To complete a diagram of your network (see the spider-web configuration on the next page), systematically consider each of the contexts listed on the table and on

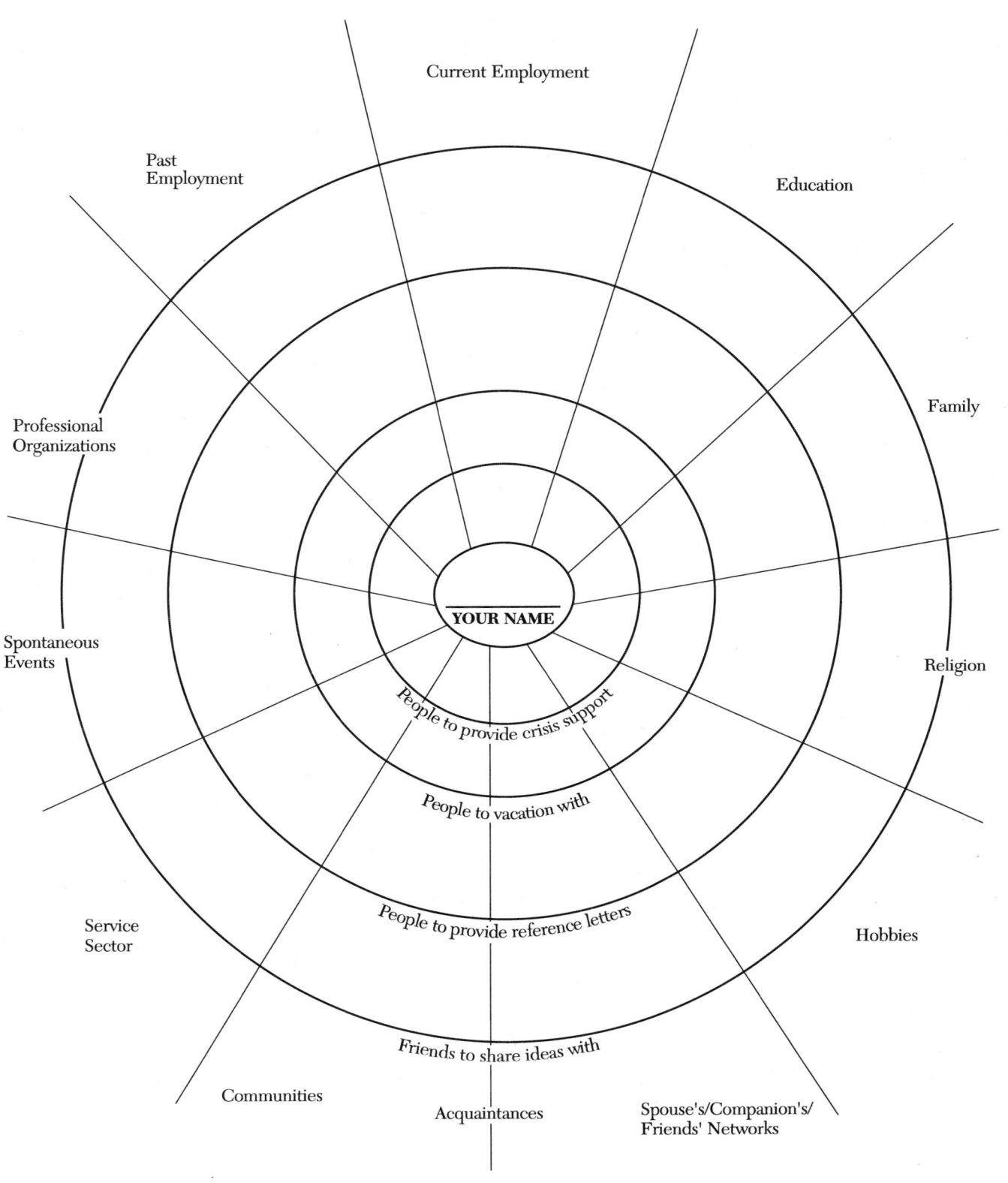

Current Employment

Past Employment

Education

Family

Professional Organizations

Religion

Spontaneous Events

Service Sector

Hobbies

Communities

Acquaintances

Spouse's/Companion's/ Friends' Networks

YOUR NAME

People to provide crisis support

People to vacation with

People to provide reference letters

Friends to share ideas with

the diagram. (Refer also to the list of contexts that appears earlier in this chapter, which gives much greater detail.) Write the names or initials of people in the appropriate levels (the circles closer to the center of the spider web indicate greater intimacy or dependence in the relationship). Your goal is to fill in the names or initials of about three hundred people so that you can get an impression of your current network.

Here are some guidelines for completing this task:

1. Spend about ten minutes per "context." Start first with your family. You might spend about ten minutes per day over the next week creating your diagram. (As you are working, you can go on and read the other chapters in this book.) After family, consider education.

2. If you cannot remember people's names but can "see their faces," indicate each with a check mark. Later you will remember, and then you can record their names or initials.

3. Duplicate entries of names are fine. For example, if you and your dad both belong to the Rotary, add your dad under both "Family" and "Professional Organizations."

4. Be patient. This process takes time—time that you will find is well invested. If you get stuck trying to come up with people who belong in the inner circles, consider starting with the outermost circle and working your way in.

5. Approximately a week after you have completed your spider-web diagram, review it and add anyone you have forgotten or overlooked.

6. Think about people who used to be in your network but are not there now. Do this for each of the categories: acquaintances, friends to share ideas with, people to provide reference letters, people to vacation with, and people to provide crisis support. Use the space that follows to list any whom you would like to have in your network again. Think about why they are not in your network now.

SETTING GOALS FOR NETWORKS AND NETWORKING

Your network and networking should be related to your goals, your support system, and your access to power and influence. By applying the following six criteria, you can assess whether this is the case and determine areas in which you might want to improve your network and networking:

1. *Crisis criterion.* Most specialists in stress and stress management recommend that you have a support system that you can count on no matter what. The authors suggest having at least four people from a variety of sources. According to Meichenbaum (1983), research suggests that individuals who can cope most effectively tend to have a variety of support systems.

2. *Enjoyment criterion.* Life should be enjoyed to the fullest. You should have at least three people with whom to share activities that you enjoy. Often these people are in the "hobbies" section of people's networks.

3. *Goals criterion.* Whatever your goals in life, your chances of achieving them and getting things done are greater when others work with you and help you. Your network should include at least twelve people who know you at the reference level. They may be inside or outside your workplace.

4. *Inverse criterion.* In the context of your current work, you should know at least as many people below you in the corporate structure as above. These people enable you to get things done effectively at work. For example, they might be technicians, secretaries, librarians, mail-delivery people, and word-processing people. In the section of your network related to work, reflect on the ratio of people below you and above you.

5. *Organizational power-broker criterion.* In your organization you should have a close ally who knows the organizational culture, who plays a role in dictating and controlling that culture, who has a political sense of the attitudes of people in power, and who is aware of how to use the processes and procedures to gain approval.

6. *Corporate stakeholder-identifier criterion.* You should know one or more people in your organization who can identify those who have a stake in any issue that you wish to promote. A "stakeholder" is someone who has to change his or her job or behavior in some way so that a new policy can be implemented. For example, if you think parking around your office building should be limited, then any employee who drives a car to work becomes a stakeholder because he or she is affected. People who can identify stakeholders for you usually have been with the company a long time and are astutely aware of the culture as well as most employees' concerns and turfs.

Stakeholders come from all parts of the organization and may have very different stances on any issue. Some might feel that your goal is a good one, that achieving it would help them; others might oppose you; still others might be indifferent or neutral toward your goal.

———————————— ┼┼┼ ————————————

✍ *Activity 8. Assessing Your Current Network*

Below is a brief summary of people that your network should include, according to the six preceding criteria. Check the spider-web diagram of your network and identify all these people. Write their names or initials in the spaces following the numbered items. If you cannot identify the proper number of people (and who they are) for each criterion, make some notes to indicate which areas of your network you need to work on.

1. At least four people, from a variety of sources, whom you can count on during a crisis

2. At least three people with whom to share activities that you enjoy

3. At least twelve people who can help you achieve your goals and get things done

4. At least as many people below you in the organizational hierarchy as above you

5. At least one organizational power broker

6. At least one stakeholder identifier

Areas To Improve

SUMMARY

People work better as a result of having goals. Your goals should be written, be broken down into milestones, include criteria, be consistent with your lifetime objectives, and be achievable. To achieve a goal, usually you will require some support.

In this chapter you learned how to create a spider-web diagram of your network by identifying people who can provide you with support in time of crisis, people with whom you can spend a two-week vacation or holiday, people who know you well enough to supply a reference letter (so you can reach your goals), friends with whom you can share ideas, and acquaintances. You learned that this range of people exists in the contexts of family, education, work, professional organizations, spontaneous events, the service sector, the communities in which you presently live and used to live, your spouse's/companion's/friends' networks, hobbies, and religion.

You also learned that you can assess whether your network and the way you go about the process of networking are appropriate in terms of helping you reach your personal goals, supplying support and encouragement, and providing access to power and influence.

From your assessment you can determine which areas of your network need improvement.

———————— ┼┼┼ ————————

✍ Activity 9. Discoveries from Chapter 2

In the space provided, write what you have discovered as a result of reading and working through this chapter. Add how you might apply the discovered ideas in your daily living.

Discovery	Application
Goal setting	
Your personal goals	
Spider-web diagram of network	
Criteria for assessing networks	

Discovery	Application
Goals for networking	
Other	

---|-|-|-|-|---

✍ Activity 10. Action Plan for the Next Month

Identify one area from the discoveries activity that you want to work on. Create an action plan for the next month for improving in that area. Track your progress by jotting down notes.

Goal:

Criteria:

Support needed:

Progress and evidence:

3

SKILLS FOR EFFECTIVE NETWORKING

OVERVIEW OF THIS CHAPTER

Networking is something that people do regardless of their interpersonal skills. However, to improve the effectiveness of your networking, you should develop the skills required for effective interaction with others.

In this chapter you will reaffirm the required attitude toward networking—a genuine interest in others. You will learn about the role of self-awareness in interacting effectively with others. You will also become acquainted with the fundamental human rights and the guidelines for "interpersonal Shangri-la." In addition, you will become familiar with a model for developing trust and warmth and the implications of this model.

SELF-AWARENESS AND NETWORKING

There is an important linkage between self-awareness and networking. Self-awareness leads to self-acceptance, and self-acceptance allows you to accept others. Accepting yourself and others is essential if you are to develop trust in your relationships, and trust is the critical element in networking.

Accepting yourself means learning to be yourself, without denying or suppressing the unique characteristics that set you apart from others. Trying to be liked by everyone or to behave as others want you to behave is counterproductive; no matter what you do or how hard you try, some people will be displeased. But when you accept yourself for what you are and are proud of yourself, most people will feel comfortable around you; they will know that they can associate with you without feeling a sense of strain.

One possible indicator of your self-image is your "self-talk," the things you say to yourself about yourself. If you typically say negative things to yourself, the chances are that your self-image is negative. Positive self-comments, in contrast, indicate a positive self-image. Even when you make a mistake, you can respond negatively with a self-comment such as "Now that was a stupid thing to do," or you can respond positively with a self-comment such as "That's good; I've learned something. The next time I'll get it right."

Your self-talk has as much effect on the outcome of your efforts as the comments of others. If you use positive self-talk, over time you will believe in yourself and you will increase the likelihood of success in whatever you do. But if you give yourself nothing but negative messages, tasks will seem impossible, problems will seem insurmountable, and you will reduce the likelihood of success.

Activity 11. Practicing Positive Self-Talk

Monitor your self-talk for the next week. What does your self-talk suggest about your image of yourself? If you find that you tend to use a lot of negative self-talk, be proactive. During the following week, concentrate on making positive comments to yourself.

Morrison et al. (1987, p. 33) identify "easy to be around" as one of six significant characteristics of successful people. Here are some ways to make yourself "easy to be around":

- Cultivate the qualities that you like in yourself.

- Learn to enjoy being alone.

- Develop your capacity for pleasure.

- Be positive, smile; avoid cynicism.

- Believe in yourself.

- Be ready to confront people when you disagree with them about something that matters to you. Be assertive. State your feelings and opinions in a way that is not insulting.

- Remember that you are what you create.

How To Develop Self-Awareness

There are a number of ways to develop self-awareness. One way is to ask your significant other, friends, acquaintances, and co-workers for feedback regarding the impact of your behavior on them. Try to ask specific questions about specific behaviors; otherwise being questioned in this manner can be overwhelming or threatening to people. For example, you might want to ask about one or more of these issues:

- Your listening skills;

- Your ability and willingness to state your position on an issue;

- Your willingness to disclose your feelings;

- Your sensitivity to the thoughts and feelings of others;

- The way you handle anger;

- The congruence between your verbal and nonverbal behavior (the consistency between your body language and what you are saying);

- Your ability and willingness to take risks;

- Your level of participation in problem-solving meetings; and

- Your helpfulness to new staff members (in terms of answering their questions, helping them to understand policies and procedures, and so on).

You can encourage people to give you honest feedback by reacting nondefensively to what they say and not rationalizing the behavior being discussed, by paraphrasing what they say to indicate your understanding of the information, and by expressing your thoughts and feelings about the information (Bushardt & Fowler, 1989). Always express your thanks for the feedback. (See also item 8 under "Follow the Guidelines for 'Interpersonal Shangri-la'" in this chapter.)

You can receive feedback not only from people but also from instruments or questionnaires designed to increase self-awareness, such as the Myers-Briggs Type Indicator, the Personal Style Inventory, the Life-Style Questionnaire, the Personality Traits Inventory, the Work-Needs Assessment Inventory, the Behavior Description, The Cognitive-Style Inventory, The Visibility/Credibility Inventory, and the Networking Skills Inventory.[2] In addition, here are some other ways in which you can increase your self-awareness:

- Ask a friend or mentor to observe your behavior at social gatherings or at meetings and to share observations with you afterward.

- Contract with a friend or co-worker to develop a particular skill that you want to obtain. Meet regularly with this person to discuss your progress and to ask for observations and advice. In the course of obtaining the skill and sharing your experiences with your friend or co-worker, you will learn much about yourself.

---

[2]The first of these instruments, the Myers-Briggs Type Indicator, may be obtained from Consulting Psychologists Press, 3803 E. Bayshore Rd., Palo Alto, California 94303, phone (415) 969-8901. The remaining instruments are from Pfeiffer & Company's *Annuals* and *Handbooks* and may be obtained by writing, phoning, or faxing any of Pfeiffer & Company's offices. (See the copyright page of this book for the address, phone number, and fax number of the San Diego office.)

- Set personal goals for yourself and review them regularly. Your goals will give you valuable information about yourself.

- Review the personal and work-related decisions you have made in the last few months. Decisions are an excellent indicator of personal tendencies and preferences.

- Examine your "to-do" or activities lists or your calendar for the past several weeks or months. How you spend your time is an indication of what you value and what your priorities are.

All of these methods are effective. You may want to combine several of them to increase your self-knowledge. Whatever you learn about yourself will make you a better networker. In fact, Covey (1989) emphasizes that developing your own self-awareness and self-confidence is a prerequisite to improving your interactions with others.

USING INTERPERSONAL SKILLS TO NETWORK EFFECTIVELY

To network effectively, you need to show empathy, understanding, and genuineness in your interactions with others. You must learn to understand and accept the viewpoints of others, even if you disagree with them; and you must accept others as individuals. Similarly, you must make your own thoughts and feelings known, and you must promote recognition of yourself as an individual. According to Morrison et al. (1987, p. 171), the third commandment for success is "help others to help you." The following paragraphs explain how to create the kind of interactions that promote empathy, understanding, and genuineness.

Network To Help Others As Well As Yourself

Your underlying motive for networking should be a genuine interest in people. The one and only rule of networking is not to create a network for the sole purpose of exploiting it for your own gain. If you network for selfish reasons alone, your network will fail. A network survives and functions on the basic premise that there is mutual respect and interest among the people in that network. The authors approach networking with the philosophy that their lives are enriched by giving to others.

Honor the Fundamental Human Rights

Cawood (1988), H. Langsford (personal communication, 1984), and Rhode (1989) summarize the fundamental personal rights that all of us have:

1. We have the right to be respected by others (to feel good about ourselves and to be treated fairly).

2. We have the right to have needs and to have those needs be as important as other people's needs. Moreover, we have the right to ask (not demand) that other people respond to our needs and to decide whether we will take care of another person's needs.

3. We have the right to have feelings and to express those feelings in ways that do not violate the dignity of others (the right to feel tired, happy, silly, sexy, depressed, lonesome, and so on).

4. We have the right to decide whether we will meet other people's expectations or act in ways that suit us better, provided we act so that we do not violate other people's rights. (We have the right to say "no" to people without feeling guilty, and we have the right to decide how we want to respond to others. We also have the right to change our minds, to say that we do not know, and to ask for information from experts.)

5. We have the right to form our own opinions and to express those opinions.

There is one condition: *We may not exercise any of these rights by violating or infringing on the rights of others.*

In applying the fundamental human rights, start with yourself. Begin with self-acceptance, which is the unconditional belief in your inherent worth regardless of your successes and failures. Then add self-respect, which is the pride obtained from honest, enthusiastic efforts at some endeavor that seems worth doing. Self-respect has nothing to do with results and rewards; it comes from your efforts and, therefore, is within your own control. For more information on self-acceptance and self-respect, see Rusk and Rusk (1988).

Follow the Guidelines for "Interpersonal Shangri-la"

No matter what the occasion or whom you are interacting with, consider the following as general guidelines for "interpersonal Shangri-la"—effective, satisfying interpersonal relationships (based on Brothers, 1978; Covey, 1989; Johnson, 1986; Kassorla, 1984; Morrison et al., 1987; Peale, 1969; Whetten & Cameron, 1984; Ziglar, 1986):

1. Everyone is unique and is to be valued because of that uniqueness.

2. The golden rule is still golden: Treat others as you would like to be treated.

3. Look for the good in others; expect the best. Support others; cheer for them and help them to succeed. Make them look good. People do not care how much you know—just how much you care about them.

4. Do not say anything about anyone that you would not say to that person's face. Praise in public, but reprimand in private.

5. Give credit to others when it is due. Rarely will you achieve something completely on your own. Remember that if you take all of the credit (and fail to acknowledge those who helped you), no one will ever willingly help you again.

6. When you receive positive feedback, express your thanks. Do not minimize your accomplishment by saying something like "Oh, I guess I was lucky" or "It was nothing." And do not deflect it by saying "Oh, you're terrific too."

7. In general, focus your responses to be at the same level of intensity and intimacy as the other person's. (The exception occurs when the other person behaves aggressively; for example, if he or she shouts at you, do not shout back.) If someone comes to you to describe an issue that he or she is excited about, do not be too relaxed; the other person might interpret your relaxation as indifference. Similarly, if someone describes his or her innermost feelings, you might share some of yours as well.

8. When you receive negative feedback, take a deep breath and silently count to ten. You cannot improve unless you clearly understand what you are to work on. Consequently, you should repeat what you heard the other person to say; if you do not understand the context or the meaning of the comment, then ask questions for clarification only. Do not get into an argument; do not try to disprove; do not get defensive.

9. Be loyal first to yourself and then to others. Be loyal to your boss; your job is to make your boss look good. Be loyal to your peers and subordinates; your job is to make them look good. Either be loyal to your organization, or go to work for a different organization that you can support.

10. Maintain a sense of humor; keep things in perspective.

11. Earn the cooperation of others; do not demand it.

12. Approach others with Will Rogers' credo: "I never met a man I didn't like." Practice liking people.

✍ Activity 12. Interpersonal-Skills Assessment

Reflect on your attitude toward, awareness of, and skill in following guidelines 1 through 12. Use the space following and at the top of the next page to make some notes about areas in which you need to concentrate your efforts to gain needed skill.

Items 13 through 26 deal with giving feedback to another person.

13. When you give feedback to another person, focus on its value to the recipient rather than on the power or release that it provides you.

14. Focus on offering only as much information as the recipient can productively use at that time, rather than on unloading as much information as you would like.

15. When you give corrective feedback, focus on the recipient's behavior, not on his or her personality. Be problem oriented, not personality oriented. For example, say "When you arrive late for meetings, I feel frustrated because all of us have to wait to begin" instead of "You have a cavalier attitude toward meetings." The first remark makes use of a standard structure for an assertive comment: "When you...I feel...because...."

16. Describe the recipient's behavior; do not give advice or make judgments about that behavior (unless, because of your position, you must provide a judgment). Even when you are asked for advice, it usually is better to help the recipient explore options than to give your solution to the problem.

17. Focus on your observations rather than your inferences, interpretations, conclusions, or judgments. Talk about what was said and done, not about your speculations regarding the recipient's motivation.

18. Describe the recipient's behavior in terms that place him or her on a continuum between "low" and "high" or "large" and "small" rather than in terms of "either/or." For example, participation in problem-solving meetings may be "low," "high," or at any point between.

19. Show ownership of the ideas, opinions, and feelings that you state; use "I" rather than "some people" or "we."

20. Cite a specific situation rather than an abstract behavior (for example, "leaving last week's staff meeting to make a phone call" rather than "your indifference in meetings").

21. Discuss only events that happened in the very-recent past. Do not engage in recriminations for behaviors that occurred in the distant past.

22. For every two areas that you would like the recipient to work on, identify five things at which he or she is performing satisfactorily (two to work on; five "warm fuzzies").

23. Be equality oriented rather than superiority oriented.

24. Never shout, pound the table, use foul language, or wage personal attacks.

25. Carefully consider the time and the place for giving feedback. Remember that the recipient must be ready for the feedback.

26. Provide positive feedback often, honestly, and as soon as possible after the noteworthy event. Norman Vincent Peale (1969, p. 200) suggests, "Never miss an opportunity to say a word of congratulation upon anyone's achievement, or express sympathy in sorrow or disappointment."

--------------------------------- ┠╂┨ ---------------------------------

✍ Activity 13. Designing Appropriate Responses

Each of the following comments represents an inappropriate response. Refer to guidelines 13 through 26 and use the space provided to the right of each comment to write an appropriate response. Remember the basics: focus on behavior; avoid advice or judgments; talk about your observations; avoid speculating about motivation; place the behavior on a continuum; show ownership with "I" comments; avoid abstractions.

"You're incompetent."

"Why can't you ever turn in your work on time?"

"You have about a million little habits that drive your co-workers crazy."

"That's just like the ridiculous idea you had for last year's Christmas party."

"You never help around the house."

"You don't listen to me."

"You're never there for me when I need you."

———————— ┼┼┼ ————————

Use Covey's (1989) Model of Trust

As mentioned previously, trust is the critical element in networking. Johnson (1986, p. 52) says that trust "reduces your own and the other person's fears of betrayal and rejection and promotes the hope of acceptance, support, and confirmation." Covey (1989) offers a model of trust that the authors find useful in terms of building and improving a network. He sees trust as an "emotional bank account" that you build up within a person with whom you share a relationship. When the account balance is high, trust is high. When the account is overdrawn, trust is low.

To build up a trust account through deposits, you:

• Keep your commitments to yourself and to others.

- Clarify the expectations that you have of yourself and of others.

- Show personal honesty, integrity, and loyalty to others, especially when they are not present.

- Promptly and sincerely apologize when you know you are wrong.

- Honor the fundamental human rights and follow the guidelines for interpersonal Shangri-la.

- Take time to see things from other people's perspectives. Show that you seek to understand them. Empathize with them; see the world through their individual frames of reference. This means that although you may not agree with other people, you accept them as they are, "warts and all."

When you make deposits in this way, you risk being exploited, ridiculed, or rejected. But trust develops when the deposits are graciously accepted, and it further develops when others reciprocate.

You withdraw from a trust account when you:

- Ask a favor.

- Ask people to do something your way, even though they disagree.

- Ask others to give up some of their own fundamental human rights.

The authors extend Covey's (1989) model of an "emotional bank account" to an "emotional-warmth bank account." "Warmth" is the enjoyment of each other's company. You make a deposit in a warmth account when you behave in a thoughtful and considerate fashion and you listen. You withdraw from a warmth account when you use listening as a one-way street—when you expect to be listened to, but you never ask about the other person.

Although trust is essential in all relationships in your network, warmth is not. Generally warmth is found in the more intimate circles of your network (see p. 17.) For example, there is probably great warmth in the relationships you share with people who provide you with crisis support. Similarly, there needs to be warmth in the relationship if you are to vacation with a person. However, at the reference level, you need trust but not warmth. Consequently, you can have trust without warmth in a relationship but not vice versa.

SUMMARY

The required attitude toward networking is a genuine interest in others. But as Covey (1989) suggests, you need to manage yourself before you can act effectively on your interest in others by managing your relationships with them. Through self-awareness you come to accept yourself and others, and this acceptance leads to the development of trust—a critical element in networking.

This chapter offered you a chance to reflect on your self-acceptance and described ways to develop self-awareness. It also introduced you to the fundamental human rights and the guidelines for "interpersonal Shangri-la." Finally, the authors recommended using Covey's (1989) model of trust in building relationships: Treat trust as an emotional bank account with another person, building up that account by accepting the person and by being honest, reliable, and courteous.

As you worked through this chapter, you might have identified areas that you wish to develop. If so, set goals, identify milestones, and create measurable criteria that will let you know when you have achieved each milestone. Consider keeping a journal. You also might want to ask for feedback from a close friend. Realize that there will be setbacks, and remember to call on your network for support. Take the process of personal development one day at a time. Celebrate each accomplishment, no matter how small, and learn from each disappointment.

✍ Activity 14. Discoveries from Chapter 3

Write what you have discovered as a result of reading and working through this chapter. Add how you might apply the discovered ideas in your daily living.

Discovery	**Application**
Self-awareness and networking	
Network to help others as well as yourself	
Fundamental human rights	

Discovery	Application
Guidelines for interpersonal Shangri-la	
Covey's (1989) model of trust	
Other	

———————— ┃┃┃ ————————

✍ Activity 15. Action Plan for the Coming Week

Identify one area from the discoveries activity that you want to work on. Create an action plan for the next week for improving in that area. Use the following space to record notes about your plan and your progress.

4

Principles of Effective Networking

OVERVIEW OF THIS CHAPTER

In this chapter you will learn the six principles of effective networking, and you will practice applying them in activities that will help you in your networking efforts.

Here are the six principles:

1. Excel at what you do.
2. Be nurturing and supportive to others.
3. Know many different kinds of people (with diverse interests and backgrounds).
4. Be visible; join and participate in various groups.
5. Learn other people's unique qualities.
6. Be organized.

EXCEL AT WHAT YOU DO

It is essential to excel at what you do. You cannot replace competence with networking. The basics of producing excellent efforts are as follows:

1. Be accountable; keep your word.
2. Meet the expectations of others.
3. Be reliable; do your work on time and within budget.
4. Be accurate; do your work right the first time.
5. Follow through.
6. Anticipate problems and develop contingency plans.
7. Set and prioritize goals.

1. Be Accountable; Keep Your Word

Realize that it is completely within your control to do what you say you will do. Obviously, there are going to be times when you feel that you have too much to do:

an overflowing in-basket, numerous memos to write, follow-up tasks to perform for customers, budget requests to analyze, and so on and so on. Often you may feel that you could not finish everything even if you worked twenty-four hours a day. When that is the case, what do you do? You create personal guidelines for being accountable and you adhere to those guidelines.

When you are pinched for time, remember that you may not have to meet every need *in the way you originally planned.* For example, you may not have time to dictate a formal letter, have someone type it, and then proofread the finished product; but you may have time to hurriedly write the important information yourself and then fax it. Here are some other strategies that you might consider as guidelines for staying accountable, especially when time is a problem:

- Check to make sure that everything does, in fact, need to be done. (Occasionally you will find that circumstances have changed since you received an assignment and that the task no longer has to be completed.)

- Ask for someone's help in doing part or all of a task.

- Renegotiate deadlines.

————————————— ╫ ————————————

✍ *Activity 16. Establishing Guidelines for Being Accountable*

Use the following space to record personal guidelines that you will use to stay accountable.

————————————— ╫ ————————————

2. Meet the Expectations of Others

Do what your job description dictates—and then some. Try to think of your tasks from the point of view of your "customers" (your supervisor, your co-workers, the company's external clients, and so on). What would they want? What would your customers think were some extra courtesies that you could perform in addition to what is expected of you? Joel Weldon (1982) suggests that we give people more than they think they are worth.

————————————— ╫╫╫ —————————————

✍ Activity 17. Duties and Activities

Here are the instructions for completing this activity:

1. Make a copy of the following table. The original is for you to fill out, and the copy is for your supervisor to fill out.

2. In the left column of the following table, list the duties and activities for which you are responsible, according to your job description. Then complete the right column with the duties and activities that you actually perform. Review the two columns and make notes about any discrepancies: (1) tasks that your job description mentions but you do not perform and (2) tasks that you perform but your job description does not mention.

3. Give the blank copy of the table to your supervisor and ask him or her to complete Step 2, comparing the duties and activities in your job description with the ones you actually perform and noting discrepancies.

4. Meet with your supervisor to compare the completed tables. Make sure you identify any duties and activities from your job description that you have been neglecting so that you can start attending to them. Also check the tasks you have been performing that do not appear on your job description. Your objective is to "go the extra mile" in ways that your supervisor perceives as useful. If your supervisor sees no benefit in the extra tasks you have been performing, then you and your supervisor might want to discuss "extras" that will be seen as beneficial.

5. If you wish, you can take this activity a step further and compare expectations about your job with other customers (people whose needs you must meet, whether those people are external to the company or fellow employees). In this way you can determine how to meet the needs of the people you serve in your job and how to "go the extra mile" for them. After you have identified extras, think of any "stakeholders" who might feel you were encroaching on their turf if you performed these extras; then consider options you might take if you wanted to go ahead with your plans.

DUTIES AND ACTIVITIES

Duties and Activities
From Job Description

Duties and Activities
Actually Performed

Notes on Discrepancies/Extras:

––––––––––––– ┼┼┼ –––––––––––––

3. Be Reliable—on Time and Within Budget

Do your work on time and within budget. If possible, do it ahead of schedule and under budget. Meet deadlines. Start meetings on time.

Part of being reliable is having the right attitude, and part is managing time appropriately. You must have the attitude that you want to be punctual in all that you do. Joel Weldon (1982) says that if you are not early, you are late. He goes on to suggest that the greatest time wasters are these:

- The telephone;
- Crisis management;
- Unclear objectives;
- Lack of priorities;
- Poor planning;
- Drop-in visitors;
- Ineffective delegation;
- Doing too much;
- Going to meetings;
- Being disorganized;
- The inability to say "no";
- Procrastination;
- A messy desk; and
- Paperwork.

Time management and "learning to say no" are two issues that impact on your ability to excel at what you do. Time management is based on having personal goals. Once you know what your goals are, you can prioritize them. What you do should move you toward achieving your goals.

Many books are available on time management (Bliss, 1976; Covey, 1989; Lakein, 1973; MacKenzie, 1975; Taylor, 1981). If you need help in managing your time so that you can be more reliable, consult one of these sources.

4. Be Accurate—Do It Right the First Time

Do your work right the first time. Check and double-check before you release your work. Compose your own "standards of performance" and make sure you adhere to those standards.

✍ Activity 18. Standards of Performance

Write down your personal "standards of performance." Consider whether you have a set of standards that applies to all tasks, specific standards that apply to specific responsibilities, or both.

Standards for All Tasks

Standards for Specific Tasks

Task   *Standard*

5. Follow Through

For many, if not most, activities, we must rely on others to finish the task by reproducing and mailing materials and so forth. Therefore, after you have completed any task, you must make sure that the finished product arrived at its destination—that those you depended on to duplicate, deliver, explain, or whatever did their jobs.

✍ Activity 19. People Who Assist

The following are instructions for completing this activity:

   1. In the following space list all the people whom you depend on to get things done and whose work reflects on you. Then prioritize these people in terms

of whom you depend on the most (the person you depend on most will be numbered 1, the next person 2, and so on).

2. Consider a recent task for which you had to depend on the assistance of others. How might you have made sure that they did their jobs without appearing to have been "checking up" on them?

----------------- ┼┼┼ -----------------

6. Anticipate Problems; Develop Contingency Plans

Often the unexpected prevents us from doing our jobs well. Consequently, for each task or project that you work on, you should anticipate what might go wrong and develop contingency plans. If you make such plans and things do indeed go wrong, you can carry out your plans and succeed in spite of problems. You also need to anticipate where you, your job, and the organization are going and prepare appropriately.

Kepner and Tregoe (1965) call this approach "potential problem analysis." First you list all the events that might have an adverse effect on your work. Then you assess the probability or likelihood of each, using a scale from 0 (very unlikely) to 10 (extremely likely), as well as the seriousness of the event if it does happen, using a scale from 0 (not serious) to 10 (extremely serious). Finally, you multiply the probability of each event by its seriousness to determine the rankings of the various events. (The event with the highest number becomes the first-ranked event, the event with the next-highest number becomes the second-ranked event, and so on).

Subsequently, you address the first-ranked event by developing contingency plans and options. Then you develop plans and options for the second-ranked event, and then the third, and so on until you have plans for all events. Figure 2 offers one example of potential problem analysis for giving a talk to supervisors. For other examples, see Kepner and Tregoe (1965) and Arnold (1978).

Action: <u>Give a talk to supervisors</u>

Potential Problems	Likeli-hood	Serious-ness	Likeli-hood x Serious-ness	Rank	Possible Solutions
Lose transparencies	1	8	8	6	Send paper "reprints" and transparencies ahead of time and check their arrival.
Show up at wrong time or place	2	10	20	2	Mark in calendars at work and home. Have someone phone me. Double-check time and place.
No overhead projector or screen	2	8	16	3	Recheck that projector and screen have been ordered. Make paper "reprints" of slides.
Power failure	1	8	8	5	Make paper "reprints."
Bad news received by supervisors just before meeting	3	10	30	1	Schedule meeting to take place *before* budget is released. Include possible part in talk about "bad news."
Plane strike or delay	1	10	10	4	Go a day early. Have a local presenter available.

Figure 2. Potential Problem Analysis for Giving a Talk to Supervisors[3]

---
[3] Based on Kepner and Tregoe (1965).

✍ Activity 20. Potential Problem Analysis

Create a potential problem analysis for a task or project that you are currently working on.

Action: _____

Potential Problems	Likeli-hood	Serious-ness	Likeli-hood x Serious-ness	Rank	Possible Solutions

7. Set and Prioritize Goals

Prepare yourself for the future by setting personal goals, prioritizing those goals, and adding roles to your current position so that you get a chance to develop the skills you will need.

BE NURTURING AND SUPPORTIVE TO OTHERS

People will seek you out if you:

- Are optimistic and positive;

- Are a good listener;

- Are a good speaker and, therefore, can be an effective spokesperson for the ideas of others;

- Nurture an environment in which others can succeed and do well;

- Show a genuine interest in others;

- Are discreet, protecting the confidentiality of the personal information that others share with you; and

- Do not promise more than you can deliver.

KNOW MANY DIFFERENT KINDS OF PEOPLE

Your network should include many people with diverse interests and backgrounds. Moreover, you should not think that because you meet a person socially, that person cannot be important to you professionally. Every person you meet can be important to you in some way and should be included in your network.

You do not have to meet people to start developing your network. For example, if you have to contact many people in different companies, keep a collection of notices of job appointments from professional publications. In this way, if you have to contact a particular company, you can consult your collection and come up with the name of a contact and some sense of the person's background.

Also keep a current stock of professional directories, lists of people who have attended workshops with you, and a file of business cards. You might consider using double entries to aid retrieval.

Start thinking of your various life activities as opportunities for networking. For example, suppose you are planning a ski trip to Switzerland. What preparations would you make in order to get the most from the trip from a networking standpoint? What follow-up might be appropriate? Your preparations might include checking to see if you know anyone in that area, including pilots who fly there; stocking up on business cards to take with you; becoming familiar with the area; thinking of skiers you met in other locations; learning about businesses in the ski area; and educating yourself about Swiss "hot-tub" etiquette.

Think about what you might do, experience, and anticipate. If your trip is to be a package plan, request a list of your fellow travelers in advance. Anticipate that these people might enjoy parties or celebrations. What would you need to bring with you if you were to offer to organize a party after you got there?

Follow-up is equally important. After the ski trip, send thank-you letters, organize the information you obtained, write people's names on the backs of your photographs, and send duplicates of the photographs to your new friends. Some people you met may have asked you to send them information—details about another ski resort, for example. Honor such requests and send the information promptly.

BE VISIBLE

Being visible does not mean that you have to be in the limelight; however, people should know of your group or organizational affiliations. Being visible starts in very small ways. For instance, you become visible when you respond correctly to compliments—by saying "Thank you" rather than "Oh, it was nothing" or "I was lucky." To accomplish visibility, you might assume responsibility for a small task and then do it extremely well. You might agree to be a spokesperson. Also, remember and use people's names when you see them.

Write to your alma mater about newsworthy events and accomplishments that concern you. Send notices of changes and achievements to the appropriate professional journals. Identify your areas of specialization and then write articles and offer to present speeches on related topics. The focus of such articles and speeches should be how others might benefit, not how great your achievement is.

Within an organization you become visible by doing "extra" things and by reinforcing correct behavior in the people you supervise (not by going over the boss's head or by being obstructive). Whetten and Cameron (1984, p. 256) suggest that we can be visible by "hand delivering our reports," and Morrison et al. (1987, p. 170) state that one of the commandments for success is to "be seen as being able."

If you move to a new neighborhood, get to know your neighbors. Regardless of your situation, your neighbors are vital in your network: They can keep an eye on your house when you are away, and they can lend you things or provide help during emergencies. One approach you might take is to invite them to a potluck supper. Supply name tags and perhaps even color code the tags according to the side of the street that people live on or some other criterion that will help you remember and place people. Gather information from your guests when you invite them. Supply a map showing locations and names of neighbors. You might ask each neighbor to bring a slide showing a favorite person or place; then, at the potluck, you can show the slides and give people a chance to share information about their slides.

Here are more ideas for building visibility in a positive way, all contributed by people who have used the material in this book:

- Do volunteer work;

- Wear bright colors;

- Use a strong handshake;

- Place fresh flowers on your desk at work every Monday;

- Keep a name plate on your desk at work;

- Make eye contact with people;

- Smile and call people by name;

- Put magnetic car panels on your car to identify your business;

- Use a personalized automobile license plate;

- Install a fax machine in your home;

- Learn to say "no" when appropriate; and

- Write letters to the editor of a local newspaper.

———————— ✚✚✚ ————————

✍ Activity 21. Ways To Build Visibility

In the space that follows, list ideas that you might use to build your own visibility.

———————— ✚✚✚ ————————

LEARN OTHER PEOPLE'S UNIQUE QUALITIES

Networking means more than shaking hands with everyone you meet or collecting business cards at every opportunity. You need to learn about the unique qualities of other people. Here is some of the information that you might want or need to know about others:[4]

- Name and nickname;
- Home (where he or she lives; owns or rents);
- Status (married or single);
- Formal education (how much, where);
- Work experience (where, type of work);
- Outside hobbies and activities;
- Health (disabilities, problems);
- Children (names, ages, achievements);
- Religion—background and present affiliation;
- Politics—preference and activities;
- Attitudes (toward company, boss, union);
- Problems outside the plant;
- Friends at the plant;
- Financial situation;
- Ambitions and goals;
- War experience;
- Personality (introvert, extrovert);
- Intelligence;
- Birthday;
- Date of employment;
- Social and cultural background; and
- Continuing education (seminars, workshops, and so on).

Such information is crucial, for example, if you are to send greetings or make phone calls for birthdays and other special events or to congratulate people on their accomplishments. It is also vital when you are trying to understand other people's perspectives on issues and when you are trying to achieve a win-win collaboration. For example, if you know that a colleague at work has a high mortgage that consumes a large percentage of her take-home pay, then you also know that any suggestion about work sharing is going to be very threatening to her. When you know such

---

[4]From *How To Manage Change Effectively* (p. 114) by D.L. Kirkpatrick, 1985, San Francisco: Jossey-Bass. Reprinted with permission.

information, you can be more effective in relating to people and communicating with them. Consequently, you should identify a way that is comfortable for you to obtain such information from people in your network.

Important knowledge about others is not the only benefit to be gained from conversing beyond the chit-chat level. We can also uncover interesting information about ourselves. Cawood (1988) suggests that we assertively refer to our occupations by describing ourselves in action and by removing negative value judgments. For example, when asked what you do for a living, you can resist the temptation to respond by giving your job title ("I'm an administrator"). Instead, you might describe a current challenge: "I'm developing a new course on networking."

Activity 22. Assertively Introducing Yourself

You meet a person at a conference and she asks, "What do you do?" Think of a response that *describes you in action* and that *does not add a value judgment* like "My job is boring right now...."

You will also find that if you are forthcoming and assertive in describing yourself, you encourage others to be forthcoming and assertive, too.

BE ORGANIZED

If you still have your old school yearbooks, lists of birthdays of people from your past, and lists of the names of participants in conferences and workshops that you have attended—and you have not yet added names from these sources to your spider-web diagram of your network (p. 17)—use such items now to increase your network. If you have thrown out such items, start anew by deciding how you can become organized to facilitate networking: how you will put names to faces, how you will remember crucial information about people, and how you will refresh your memory about who lives in a given city.

The authors have found that collecting business cards is not sufficient. Here are some ideas generated by others who have used this book:

- Request lists of people who have attended conferences and courses with you.

- Create a binder of the names of people who have attended various courses with you; separate the names according to the year in which each course was held.

- Store your pocket diaries for potential future reference.

- If you maintain a daily work diary, keep all such diaries. Add the telephone numbers of the people who call you and notes about your conversations. Add any additional information that might be useful to you in your networking efforts. Number the pages and index the book. (This suggestion simply adds a networking dimension to good record keeping.)

- Keep a "guest" book at the office and at home.

- Keep a personal diary of major events that you attend or host, who visits you, the food you serve your visitors, the gifts you send, and which gifts are particularly liked.

——————————— ‖‖ ———————————

✍ Activity 23. Getting Organized

In the following space, write down your ideas about how you can become organized to facilitate networking.

——————————— ‖‖ ———————————

SUMMARY

Networking is based on six principles: (1) Excel at what you do; (2) be nurturing and supportive to others; (3) know many different kinds of people; (4) be visible; (5) learn other people's unique qualities; and (6) be organized. In this chapter you completed a number of activities having to do with the six principles: being accountable, meeting the expectations of others, clarifying duties and activities (and "extras"), establishing standards of performance, following through, analyzing potential problems, generating ways to build visibility, assertively introducing yourself, and getting organized.

———————————————— ┼┼┼ ————————————————

✍ Activity 24. Discoveries from Chapter 4

Write what you have discovered as a result of reading and working through this chapter. Add how you might apply the discovered ideas in your daily living.

Discovery	Application
Excel at what you do: Be accountable	
Meet others' expectations	
Clarify duties and activities	
Identify "extras"	
Establish performance standards	

Discovery	Application
Follow through	
Anticipate problems; develop contingency plans	
Set and prioritize goals	
Be nurturing and supportive	
Know many different kinds of people	
Be visible	
Learn others' unique qualities	
Be organized	
Other	

✍ Activity 25. Action Plan for the Coming Week

Select one area from the discoveries activity that you would like to work on. Devise an action plan for the coming week for improving in that area. Use the following space to record notes about your plan and your progress during the week.

5

Nurturing Your Network

OVERVIEW OF THIS CHAPTER

This chapter offers practical suggestions for nurturing a network. It is important to understand that networks are living entities; they die if they are not nurtured. Once your network has been established, there are four ways in which you can nurture it:

1. Give unstintingly to others;
2. Add personal touches to keep your network alive;
3. Learn how to support people during crises; and
4. Retrieve people who have drifted from you.

GIVE UNSTINTINGLY TO OTHERS

Your network flourishes because of the efforts you contribute to it—not because of what you draw from it. You need to be available, reliable, and generous in sharing experience and ideas and in providing support. You also must be trustworthy and discreet.

In addition, you must become an excellent listener. In your conversations focus on learning about the other person. Congratulate yourself if a conversation ends and you know a phenomenal amount about the other person while he or she knows very little about you. If the other person is successful in getting you to talk, after about

---

Activity 26. Listening to Others

Nurturing a network requires excellent listening skills. During the coming week, make a point of listening to others. Listen with the goal that after the conversation you will be able to write down the "facts" that the other person told you as well as the implications of those facts and any inferences you made. Before you speak at meetings, write down the points and opinions expressed by others.

Note that this kind of listening necessitates asking questions to clarify meaning.

---

three minutes say something like "That's enough about me. Now what about you?" To improve your listening skills, refer to Bolton (1979), Covey (1989), Johnson (1986), and Whetten and Cameron (1984).

Spend your time thinking of people who are deserving of recognition. Nominate them for awards. Keep abreast of awards that are available, gather extensive dossiers for candidates, and give the appropriate information to those who are responsible for making awards. For example, if your employer gives a "can-do" award to a worthy employee every month, make sure that someone in management knows about the special efforts of a co-worker who might be considered for this award. You will find this process of promoting the recognition of others to be extremely rewarding.

Similarly, when you receive awards and friends write to congratulate you, write back and say how much it increases your pleasure to know that others shared in that pleasure.

✍ *Activity 27. Promoting the Recognition of Others*

In the following space, list ways in which you can promote the recognition of others.

ADD PERSONAL TOUCHES TO KEEP YOUR NETWORK ALIVE

Set aside at least thirty minutes each week to nurture your network. You can use this time in a number of ways:

- Write and mail brief notes or letters.

- Congratulate people on their retirements, achievements, awards, promotions, and so on.

- Remember and send greetings, flowers, or notes to acknowledge birthdays and special events such as Christmas, Hanukkah, Valentine's Day, Secretaries' Day, and so on.

- Attend a function honoring a friend; take photographs and send copies to the person being honored.

- Show your appreciation for jobs well done. Such feedback should be direct (done in person, if possible), specific to the event, and timely (within twenty-four hours). If you are sending a letter of thanks, mail a copy to the person's supervisor, if appropriate. If you do not have time to write a letter, make a phone call or send a brief message on the computer.

- Do something personal for a friend in need or just to show that you care: Shovel snow from a friend's driveway or mow the lawn, babysit, bake something, offer to pick up dry cleaning or to run other errands, feed and care for a friend's pet while he or she is out of town, and so on.

Any of a number of small gifts are also appropriate as remembrances or expressions of gratitude: peanuts, flowers, hard candy, a pen, personalized jiffy notes, a coffee mug, a balloon arrangement, a gift certificate, personalized stationery, wine, doughnuts, Post-it™ notes that say what you like about the person, a card, home-baked items, a single chocolate placed on a person's desk, a treat for a person's pet, a colored file organizer, a miniature cosmetics kit, a travel pillow, a magnifying glass, a car compass, a dashboard holder for coffee cup or sunglasses, a business-card holder, a subscription to a magazine, a poster, a bookmark, a letter opener, a key holder, a movie pass, a luncheon certificate, a wall plaque with a message of appreciation or an inspirational message, or magazine or newspaper clippings about a subject of interest to the person. You might want to shop for or order some nonperishable gifts so that you have some handy.

Another important personal touch is to refer to people by name when you interact with them or when you pass them in the hall at work. Also keep a "guest book" at the office and at home and ask outside guests to "sign in." Say "thank you" graciously when people congratulate you, compliment you, or remember you. Finally, when you have accomplished something, let others share in both the credit and the celebration.

++++

✍ *Activity 28. Adding Personal Touches*

Consider some personal touches that you can use to keep your network thriving. Write down the names of people in your network and the details of what you might do for them to show that you care.

Name   **How I Can Show That I Care**

++++

LEARN HOW TO SUPPORT PEOPLE DURING CRISES

When crises strike others, it is sometimes difficult to figure out how to help and support them. The best approach is to contact them, let them know you care and are thinking about them, and encourage them to call on you for whatever support they need. If you have trouble figuring out what to do when a crisis hits another, consult friends in your network who are good at handling such situations and ask them for advice. The following examples offer some specific suggestions for supporting people during difficult times.

Example 1: A Friend's Spouse Dies

Raymond described his reaction to a friend's loss: "Francine is one of my closest friends. When her husband Frank died last year, I didn't do anything. I'm sure Francine understands. I just don't know what to say at funerals."

What you say at a time like this is not the important thing. Most of us do not know what to say. You cannot do the grieving for someone who has suffered a loss; but you can show that you are concerned about him or her—that you, too, share the loss. Take your cue from the grieving person; do not try to cheer the person up if he or she needs to grieve. In this case Francine needed Ray's presence. All Ray had to do was show up at the funeral, sign the registry, and shake her hand (or hug her, if appropriate). If you are involved in a situation like this and you feel you must say something at the funeral, consider comments like "I'm thinking about you" or "I'm sorry this happened."

About three weeks after the funeral it is a good idea to call the grieving person to say that he or she is in your thoughts or whatever you feel is appropriate. You might also send a card.

Example 2: Friends Divorce

Lee's close friends, Jeff and Gayle, are getting divorced. Lee likes them both. He usually goes to ball games with Jeff, and afterward he and his wife go to Jeff and Gayle's to play cards. Now that Jeff and Gayle are separated, Lee does not know what to do about the upcoming ball game. This situation is awkward for him.

Both Jeff and Gayle are going through a grieving process. Both may also be experiencing emotions such as guilt or anger. Both are in Lee's network, and both need his support. Lee should call each separately, saying how much he enjoys and wants to continue the friendship shared with that person and that he is thinking about him or her. As far as the game is concerned, Lee should retain as much of the tradition as is comfortable—probably by going to the game with Jeff but returning to his own house afterward. Lee and his wife might arrange a separate time to get together socially with Gayle.

The important thing in this situation is not to ignore or avoid either person. Instead, show support for each.

Activity 29. Offering Support

Due to a reorganization of her fifty-member department, Judy has been fired after seventeen years of service. The news about Judy has created a lot of fear in the company; many are afraid they might be next. All employees are keeping busy and maintaining a low profile. This is Judy's last week. Yesterday an appreciation party was held for her; five people showed up. You are not in her department, but you know her as an acquaintance.

What might you do?

RETRIEVE PEOPLE WHO HAVE DRIFTED FROM YOU

As you change, so will your interests and your closeness to people. Over time some people will drift from you. For example, Nicole and Mary Alice were co-workers and close friends. They called each other at least once a week, and they went to events together. Then Nicole was transferred to another city, and Mary Alice was promoted. Distance and new interests meant that they seldom touched base with each other. After about six months, Mary Alice realized that they had drifted apart.

This situation is fairly typical. If you have been promoted or have experienced events that have altered your life circumstances for the better, people who were your friends previously may be thinking that you are now "more important" and may no longer have time for them. Similarly, if one of your friends has been promoted or has received a financial windfall or something of that nature, you may be assuming that the relationship is irretrievable.

When people drift from you, you may feel that they are no longer part of your network. That is not the case, however; if someone has been in your network at any time, that person is always in your network, no matter how far he or she drifts. You must decide whether you want to retrieve the relationship and bring it closer or let it continue to drift. One approach is to contact the person and see how appropriate it is to reinstate the relationship. This approach allows you to test your own feelings as well as the other person's.

Most people worry unnecessarily about how to reestablish contact. Do not worry about how. Just do it! You may send a note or card or make a phone call to say that you are thinking of the person and wondering how things are going for him or her. Encourage the person to share information with you about his or her current situation. Let people know that you care about them, regardless of your circumstances or theirs. The opportunities to get together may change because of time, distance, or other factors; but the feelings that people have for one another remain.

———————— ┼┼┼ ————————

✍ Activity 30. Retrieving Drifters

Think of some people who have drifted from you and whose closeness you miss. Write their names in the left column below. In the right column, write the action you will take to retrieve each relationship.

Name   **Action**

———————— ┼┼┼ ————————

SUMMARY

To nurture your network, you need to (1) give unstintingly to others; (2) add personal touches; (3) support people during crises; and (4) retrieve people who have drifted.

———————————— ┼┼┼ ————————————

✍ Activity 31. Discoveries from Chapter 5

Write what you have discovered as a result of reading and working through this chapter. Add how you might apply the discovered ideas in your daily living.

Discovery	Application
Give unstintingly to others	
Add personal touches	
Support people during crises	
Retrieve people who have drifted	
Other	

✍ *Activity 32. Action Plan for the Coming Week*

Select one area from the discoveries activity that you want to work on. Devise an action plan for the coming week for improving in that area. Use the following space to record your action plan and to make notes about your progress.

6

Expanding Your Network

OVERVIEW OF THIS CHAPTER

As your goals change, your network should change, expanding to accommodate new goals. This chapter suggests ways to expand your network to make it more useful in terms of attaining your goals.

To expand your network, you should approach every party, meeting, and occasion as though you were the host or hostess. For example, if you attend church in a strange city or a meeting of a club that you have just joined, do not wait for someone to approach you; instead, introduce yourself to some people. If you find yourself alone at a party, look around and spot someone else who is alone; then approach that person and make him or her feel welcome. This technique is even more important when you are the actual host or hostess. Sondra Gotlieb's (1990, p. 5) maxim is that "a guest who does not have an enjoyable or interesting evening will not dine a second time at your table."

It is not easy to break the ice and get conversation going. If you are attending a party, you might try thinking of what the people there have in common and use that as an opener. Another idea is to volunteer to serve the hors d'oeuvres, which gives you a good opportunity to introduce yourself to others.

After you have used some kind of conversation opener, check the person's body language to see how receptive he or she is. You may want to add more details about yourself or simply ask, "How about you?" One thing that is important to remember is to be sensitive to people's needs for personal body space; do not stand too close to the person or too far away. About a foot seems to be a comfortable distance for most people.

Another suggestion for learning how to break the ice is to get together with your friends, acquaintances, and co-workers and ask them how they handle such situations. You will find that many of them have favorite conversation openers and techniques for getting another person to talk about things that matter to him or her.

MAKING YOUR NETWORK CONSISTENT WITH YOUR GOALS

Often you will find that you need to enrich your network in certain areas so that you can achieve a particular goal. (For example, as a result of completing the activities in Chapter 2, you may have uncovered such a need.) First you identify the specific goal that you plan to work on. Then you choose one of the following approaches to "diversifying"—changing your outlook, opportunities, and activities so that you can meet people and expand your network in a way that will help you reach your goal:

1. Take the initiative;
2. Seek a mentor;
3. Be a mentor;
4. Volunteer for projects or committees;
5. Chat informally in various settings;
6. Distribute and exchange business cards; and
7. Change your routine.

1. Take the Initiative

Once you have identified your goal, you may create an occasion that will bring necessary people into your network. For example, Allan Gotlieb realized that his success as Canadian Ambassador to the United States depended on his having access to high officials and members of Congress (Gotlieb, 1990). He found that these people, who would be important additions to his network, would attend his dinner parties if he also invited famous people from the arts, movies, and sports or if he arranged for the parties to be covered by the press. He also discovered that he could have a dinner in honor of an influential person—someone he wished to make part of his network—and ask for that person's suggestions of close friends to include. Thus, Gotlieb's approach was to create the occasion to fit the need.

The following examples illustrate other approaches to taking the initiative.

Using a Survey

Mike, who taught a course in design, was not well known. His goal was to assess the design approaches of others and to have access to imaginative materials and resources. He designed a survey and sent copies of it to people in 180 schools. Subsequently, he was asked to write an article based on the survey results.

He contacted one of the respondents, who was in charge of a session at a national conference, and offered to present a session at the same conference. Instead of making the presentation alone and simply summarizing his findings, he asked four other respondents to join him and make presentations. These were people who, in his judgment, contributed the most innovative approaches. After these presentations he was inundated with materials that were extremely helpful to him in his own work. Whenever he used materials contributed by others, he always acknowledged the sources.

Forming an Interest Group

Brothers (1978) describes how she expanded her network by asking three potentially interested people to her house and inviting them to join her in networking efforts. They agreed, and for the next meeting each of the four asked another potentially interested person. The group now meets once a month in a private dining room of a downtown restaurant, where they exchange mutually helpful information.

Sondra Gotlieb (1990) describes how one woman fulfilled her desire to set up a luncheon club with influential people in Washington, D.C., as members. She had contacts in the government but was retired, had no access to dining facilities, and lacked transportation and a swimming pool. The ambassadors she wanted to include in the club had dining facilities, limousines, and swimming pools but no contacts in the government. She invited the ambassadors to join the club, thus combining her strengths and needs with theirs and ultimately expanding her network.

Providing a Service and Becoming a Hub

One man needed to devise a way to keep up with the literature on the topic of problem solving. The challenge was that articles on this subject were published in a wide variety of journals. To address this challenge, he started a newsletter on the topic of problem solving. He requested that anyone interested in the subject send him reprints, articles, and information that could be published in the newsletter. This service expanded, he became well known in the subject area, and now he has a network of very influential contacts.

Sharing Expertise

Rune Olssen (personal communication, 1978) uses an effective procedure to facilitate the exchange of information. This procedure is especially helpful when used at a workshop, seminar, or some other meeting that requires people to be together for at least several hours, if not several days. First you post a sheet of newsprint with the heading "Ask Me About," and you ask all the people present to list their names and subjects about which they have expertise. Then you post a second sheet of newsprint with the heading "Please Help Me With"; you ask each person to contribute a "wish list" of skills, ideas, and information that he or she wants. You leave the lists posted prominently for the entire time that the group is assembled. People tend to consult the list often and share extensively.

2. Seek a Mentor

A mentor is a must in many aspects of life: in your organization, in your community, and in various activities and interests. A mentor is an experienced person who will pay special attention to you, look out for you, and teach you what you need to know. If you are not assigned one or if no one volunteers, invite someone to be your mentor. Cava (1988) gives excellent advice about mentors and mentoring.

3. Be a Mentor

When others in your organization look to you for guidance, give it willingly and offer information and advice about workplace traditions, norms, and expectations. Reflect on what it was like when you had your first performance appraisal, when you were first promoted to a new and more demanding position, or when you had to conduct your first performance appraisal. Offer to sit down with a person who is about to experience one of these "firsts"; listen to the person's concerns and share helpful information.

4. Volunteer for Projects or Committees

Volunteer to work on special projects or to serve on special committees. Seek advice from your mentor and from people who have a stake in these projects or the work of these committees. Do not be fooled by the names of projects or committees; understand the real power structure and volunteer for those projects or committees that will expose you to diverse people from other parts of the organization (or the community). For example, in academia, choose to be on committees that have to do with "promotion and tenure" or "curriculum and calendar" rather than on those labeled "senate" or "divisional library board."

The selection of an appropriate committee is a tricky one. Experienced networkers offer two types of feedback. Some recommend being on any committee that you are asked to serve on; they suggest that you never know where such an experience might lead. Others suggest that you reflect on your goals and ask yourself how the experience with this committee or activity will move you toward your goals. The authors' tendency is toward the latter. We suggest that you ask yourself, "Where would I like to be and what would I like to be doing four years from now? How will serving on this committee help me to reach those goals?"

5. Chat Informally in Various Settings

Spend some time chatting with people informally whenever you can. Go on coffee breaks with them and have lunch with them. Attend corporate parties, social functions, and seminars. Go to another section or department of your organization to have coffee; go to a different restaurant for lunch. Mix around. Better still, when you are in a different section or department, team up with a peer from that area.

6. Distribute and Exchange Business Cards

If your organization has not provided you with business cards, design a card and have it printed. (If you are the manager of a department in your organization, you might want to have business cards printed for all the people in your department.) The characteristics of a classy business card (as opposed to a flashy or mundane one) are that it looks appealing artistically and that the important message you want delivered is what dominates.

Look at a variety of business cards to see what features dominate. For example, you probably want your name to dominate. You might also want the name of your organization to be prominent. On your business cards, your name should appear as you want people to use it (for instance, "Don" instead of "Donald" if that is what you want people to call you). Avoid initials unless you want to be called by those initials. List your professional degrees and affiliations only if you feel that they are pertinent for general use.

Also look at business cards to see which artistic features you find appealing. Determine which design elements would get people's attention and make them respond positively.

Distribute your business cards freely and exchange them with others. When you receive a business card from someone you have just met, make notes on the back of it about what the person can do for you and vice versa. Include brief notes to help you remember the person's face and background.

A related subject is name badges. People are expected to wear name badges at many events, but the ones provided by the organizers of an event are not always good for networking purposes. Consequently, you might consider having a name badge engraved with the information you want to present. Having your own, engraved, plastic name badge is not only better for networking purposes; it also is easier to deal with than a stick-on label or a pin-on acetate holder that snags clothing. (Again, if you are a manager, you might want to have badges engraved for the people in your department.)

7. Change Your Routine

Sometimes the opportunities to meet people within an organization or formal structure are limited. This is what Allan Gotlieb, the Canadian Ambassador to the United States, found (Gotlieb, 1990). So he changed from an internal focus to an external one and concentrated on meeting people through parties held at the embassy. He changed his routine and found an alternative approach.

In another case a faculty member of a university wanted to get to know the president of that university. He found no opportunity to accomplish this goal by participating in his typical committee activities. However, he knew that the president liked to jog at a local gym, so he adjusted his recreational activities so that he could go to the same gym at the same time. Gradually he achieved his goal through informal meetings and talks at the gym.

—————————— ┠┠┠ ——————————

✎ *Activity 33. Generating Ideas for Network Expansion*

Write down ways to expand your network in the future. Consider *taking the initiative, seeking a mentor, being a mentor, volunteering for projects and committees, chatting informally in various settings, distributing and exchanging business cards,* and *changing your routine.* Be specific; link your ideas to your goals. Jot down as many ideas as you can think of; then circle or underline the best ones. If you need to develop action plans for implementing your ideas, do so.

Taking the Initiative

Seeking a Mentor

Being a Mentor

Volunteering for Projects and Committees

Chatting Informally in Various Settings

Distributing and Exchanging Business Cards

Changing Your Routine

DEVELOPING A NETWORK WHEN YOU JOIN A NEW ORGANIZATION

When you join a new organization, you are torn between two needs: to produce and to discover how to get things done (to identify the corporate attitudes and culture and to draw on the experience of the "power brokers"). If you focus only on the former, then your good ideas may be wasted. If you focus only on the latter, then you have nothing concrete to show for your time. Consequently, you need to do both.

M. Spears (personal communication, 1990) has a term for the time spent in discovering how to get things done: "naked time." Her analogy is that in your former organization you wore your old clothes, whereas in the new organization you will be putting on new clothes. While you are adjusting, though, you are naked and very vulnerable as you learn how to get things done in the new culture. She suggests that you allow yourself "naked time," using that time to listen and to observe how decisions are made.[5]

---

[5] If you are a supervisor, how much "naked time" do you allow your subordinates when they join your department/division? What opportunities do you create for them to get to know the organization and its people?

Make appointments with your peers to introduce yourself and to draw on their knowledge about the organizational power brokers and the stakeholder identifiers (see "Setting Goals for Networks and Networking" in Chapter 2). Apply the inverse criterion—get to know at least as many people below you in the corporate structure as above you (see Chapter 2). Use the organizational structure as a guide and make appointments or introduce yourself to as many key people as you can. In addition, ask the secretaries and janitors who are the key people in the organization.

For each person you contact, find out who writes his or her performance review. When you write letters acknowledging people's contributions or thanking them for their work, you will want this information so that you can send copies of your letters to their supervisors. For more suggestions on building a network in a new organization, see Black (1982) and Schiavoni (1984).

SUMMARY

There are several ways to expand your network so that you can meet your goals: Take the initiative, seek a mentor, be a mentor, volunteer for projects or committees, chat informally with people, distribute and exchange business cards, and change your routine. Also, when you join a new organization, you can expand your network by allowing yourself time to become familiar with the people and the new environment; get to know your peers, those who work above you and below you in the hierarchy, the power brokers, and the stakeholder identifiers.

———————————— **++++** ————————————

✍ Activity 34. Discoveries from Chapter 6

Write what you have discovered as a result of reading and working through this chapter. Add how you might apply the discovered ideas in your daily living.

Discovery	**Application**
Acting as a host	
Taking the initiative	
Seeking a mentor	

Discovery	Application
Being a mentor	
Volunteering for projects and committees	
Chatting informally	
Distributing and exchanging business cards	
Changing your routine	
Allowing for "naked time"	
Other	

✎ Activity 35. Action Plan for the Coming Week

Choose one area from the discoveries activity that you want to work on. Create an action plan for the coming week for improving in that area. Use the following space to make notes about your plan and your progress.

7

Coping with the "Down" Side of Networking

OVERVIEW OF THIS CHAPTER

In this chapter you will learn that the "down" side of networking has five aspects:

1. Encountering difficult behaviors;
2. Managing your commitments and saying "no";
3. Overcoming your fear;
4. Developing the patience to persevere; and
5. Dealing with ethical issues.

You will also learn some ways to cope positively with these difficulties.

ENCOUNTERING DIFFICULT BEHAVIORS

In addition to all the wonderful people you will meet in the process of networking, you will also meet some who are not so wonderful. You will encounter boors, people who will steal your ideas without giving you credit, exploiters, people who do not listen when you are talking, and others whose behavior you find obnoxious.

People whose approach to networking is to get ahead at the expense of others—exploiters and those who steal your ideas—will eventually not be a problem. Soon you will figure out their motives, and you will stay away from them. Their attitudes will be discovered, and they will be excluded not only from your network but also from the networks of others. Their own networks will dry up, leaving them with no one to exploit.

People who exhibit obnoxious behaviors but who are not out to get ahead at the expense of others—people who do not listen when you are talking, for instance—can be handled differently. Sometimes these people are unaware of their behavior—or at least of the impact of their behavior on others. When you experience obnoxious behavior, first you need to manage your own frustration and anger. Then you might want to use an assertive approach. When you act assertively, you stand up for your own rights without violating the rights of others (Kelley, 1979).

There are certain words and phrases that characterize assertive language (Kelley, 1979, p. 23): "Assertive words may include 'I' statements ('I think,' 'I feel,' 'I want'), cooperative words ('let's,' 'how can we resolve this'), and emphatic statements of interest ('what do you think,' 'what do you see')." For example, if someone appears not to be listening while you are talking, you might want to say something like "When you don't make eye contact with me, I feel frustrated and annoyed. Instead, I'd like you to look directly at me when I'm talking." Note that there is nothing aggressive or belligerent in this comment; it does not violate the other person's rights. The basic formula of this approach is to state what the person just did in specific, nonevaluative terms; to explain how that behavior made you feel; and to add what you would prefer in the way of behavior from the other person (and, if you want, how that preferred behavior would make you respond). Obviously, if the person is totally unreceptive to your assertive approach, you might want to rethink how this person fits in your network.

If you want to practice making assertive comments, try visualizing a recent situation in which you encountered obnoxious behavior. Remember what the other person said or did and how you responded. Critique your response in terms of its effectiveness. Did you deal with the situation assertively? If not, replay the situation with an assertive response. What might the other person say or do next?

Repeat this process of visualizing the situation differently until you are comfortable with your approach. Then try applying it the next time you are in a similar situation.

You can use this process for altering your responses to a number of different obnoxious behaviors. The best way to start is to apply a new approach with the least obnoxious behavior that you are likely to encounter; then you can work your way up to more obnoxious behaviors that are more difficult to deal with. With each success you will build your confidence.

MANAGING YOUR COMMITMENTS AND SAYING "NO"

You cannot do everything in the time you have available. You need to learn to say "no" and not feel guilty about it. You also need to realize that you do not need to help everyone with a 100-percent effort, by taking on all the responsibility yourself. Often you can help someone in your network by making a small effort that provides good information. For example, if someone asks you for a favor and you are unable to comply, refer him or her to another person who is less busy and/or more accomplished at completing the necessary task.

A useful guideline for prioritizing your activities is this extrapolation from Pareto's 80-20 principle: You can achieve 80 percent of a goal by making 20 percent of the effort. The key is to identify the necessary 20 percent.

Another approach is to start by saying how flattered and appreciative you are to be asked to do something, then state your concern about doing a good job, follow with the fact that in the time you have available you would not be able to meet your objectives, and finally say "no." Another approach that you might use with your supervisor is to list all the responsibilities you have now, show the list to your supervisor, and ask which task(s) can be removed from the list to make room for the new task. Naturally, your response will depend on the situation.

When you are presented with a discretionary task or responsibility, remember your major goals in life and determine whether the new task or responsibility is consistent with those goals. If it is not, you may find that saying "no" is a bit easier.

✍ Activity 36. Saying "No"

Think of some ways in which you could comfortably say "no." Write down what you might say. Come up with a variety of options that would work in different situations.

—————————— ┨┨┨ ——————————

Like any other new behavior, saying "no" becomes easier with practice. You might want to get together with a partner and do some role playing. One person plays the role of the person making a request, and the other plays the role of the person saying "no." Afterward, the person who made the request critiques the way in which the other person said "no," citing five positive features of the response and two areas to work on. Subsequently, the partners switch roles.

OVERCOMING YOUR FEAR

When you give yourself unstintingly to others, you care about them and are committed to them. The same is true of projects and proposals. When people let you down or your projects and proposals are rejected, often you feel hurt. When you commit, you risk. And when you risk, you can be disappointed. You need to enter into networking with your eyes open, knowing that you are are going to take risks, get involved, and lose some of your battles. That is the nature of networking.

There is no easy way to overcome your fear, but here are a few guidelines that you might find helpful:

- Start with small risks first—a small commitment to a person or a project. For example, go on a coffee break with a co-worker before you decide to go to a movie with him or her. If a small risk does not work out, your disappointment will not be too great. And when you succeed at small risks, you will be encouraged to take bigger risks. Work your way up to the biggest risks.

- Ask yourself, "What is the worst that could happen?" After you have imagined the most bleak scenario possible, think of ways to deal with the resulting disappointment. Being prepared can ease a lot of the sting.

- Remember that not risking is also a risk. Ask yourself, "What extraordinary opportunities might I lose if I do not take the risk? What might be the repercussions of losing those opportunities?"

DEVELOPING THE PATIENCE TO PERSEVERE

Networking requires patience. You may need to remind yourself of this fact occasionally. It takes time to develop the trust that is essential to effective networking. It takes time to build relationships and to retrieve drifters. Do not expect overnight success. Remember that you are not starting from scratch. Your network has been developing since your birth. It is already there; your task is to nurture it and to work patiently to expand it.

Stay focused on what you are gaining from your efforts. Realize that every phone call you make, every letter or note you write, every "thank-you" you utter, and potentially every interchange you have with another person is progress.

DEALING WITH ETHICAL ISSUES

As has been stated elsewhere in this book, networking is a give-and-take proposition; you will be giving much more than you take. Just as you do not want exploiters in your network, people will not want you in theirs if you take more than you give. Be sensitive to this issue; do not invite people into your network unless you are willing and able to give at least as much as you take.

Another ethical issue has to do with money—when it is appropriate to use corporate funds for networking. This is a tricky issue. If the purpose is clearly to improve "business," then the company should pay. Examples include holiday cards sent to customers and business lunches with clients. If the purpose is for you to say "thank you" to your peers or co-workers, then you should pay (for example, holiday gifts, birthday lunches, and flowers).

However, there are many situations in which the money issue is not so clear. The authors' advice is to check out such situations with your supervisor. If the organization does not have a written policy addressing the ethics of paying for lunches and so forth, then sit down with the appropriate people, talk about the issue, develop a written policy, and make sure that the policy is shared with all employees. The basic rule of thumb is that if you are in doubt, you should pay.

SUMMARY

The "down" side of networking consists of encountering difficult behaviors, managing commitments and saying "no," overcoming fear, developing the patience to persevere, and dealing with ethical issues. Anticipating these difficulties will help you to cope with them in positive ways. So will developing certain behaviors, attitudes, and policies.

--------------- ┼┼┼ ---------------

✎ Activity 37. Discoveries from Chapter 7

Write what you have discovered from reading and working through this chapter. Add how you might apply the discovered ideas in your daily living.

Discovery	Application
Encountering difficult behaviors	
Managing commitments and saying "no"	
Overcoming fear	

Discovery	Application
Developing the patience to persevere	
Dealing with ethical issues	
Other	

———————— ┼┼┼ ————————

✎ Activity 38. Action Plan for the Coming Week

Choose one area from the discoveries activity that you want to work on. Develop an action plan for the coming week for improving in that area. In the following space, write notes about what you plan to do and track your progress.

8

Drawing on Your Network

OVERVIEW OF THIS CHAPTER

There will be many times when you will want to draw on your network. On such occasions the chances are that you will receive far more from your network than you ever could anticipate.

This chapter begins by discussing the attitudes you must have if you are to draw on your network effectively. Then it presents detailed information on how to use your network for different purposes: for enjoyment, for personal growth, during crises, and to get things done. You will become aware of ways to use your network to facilitate your current activities and to get routine approval. You will also learn how to use networking to make changes: how to determine your organization's culture and values, how to identify the organization's power brokers, how to identify the stakeholders who influence the power brokers, and how to devise strategies for approaching people to get support for changes.

ESSENTIAL ATTITUDES

To use the resources of your network as effectively as possible, you need to be positive and to understand and accept the nature of change.

Be Positive—Ask

Like every other human being, you have a fundamental personal right to have needs and to ask—not demand—that other people respond to your needs. However, you cannot expect others to respond to your needs unless you approach them positively and ask for their help. The worst that can happen is that they will say "no," and you should try not to be upset when they do.

When you ask, make sure that your approach is both assertive and mannerly. Say "please." Do not call in markers for previous favors and do not apologize for asking; neither of these approaches is appropriate.

Once you have identified your need, consider a number of people in your network who might be able to help. Make sure that you have contingency plans. Never approach a person with the belief that he or she is your only resource. If you do, you might place too much pressure on that person to assist, in which case you risk damaging or ruining the relationship.

If a person is unable to help you, accept that response graciously. The person may be constrained by personal values, organizational rules, time, or other factors. Instead, try bridging (see Chapter 1): Ask the person if he or she can recommend someone who can help. If the person refers you to someone else, ask for permission to use the person's name when you contact that referred individual. If the person is unable to refer you, you might ask if he or she has suggestions about what you could do.

You can use bridging in your organization when your immediate supervisor does not have the authority to make a particular decision. Ask your supervisor who can make the decision and whether the supervisor supports your approaching that person.

Understand and Accept the Nature of Change

What To Expect from Yourself

Life is continual change. Some changes are exciting, especially those you initiate. For example, when you decide that you want to acquire a new skill and you work hard to accomplish that goal, you may feel exhilarated by your efforts. This upward, exciting path is illustrated in Figure 3 as the "champion process," meaning that during the process you are actively promoting a cause such as the acquisition of a skill or the implementation of a pet project of yours.

Other changes, especially those initiated by other people, are painful; probably you will accept them only after you have grieved for what you have lost. This path is illustrated in Figure 3 as the "grieving process."

Change is often extremely difficult, whether you see it as for the better or for the worse. Notice that both processes involve some dips in level of performance. These dips are attributable to the stress and uncertainty that accompany change, regardless of whether you initiated that change or wanted it.

Thus, the best approach to change is to understand that it involves ups and downs, accept this fact, and call on your network for support. When you are working through a change—particularly one that has been imposed—refer to Figure 3 and chart your progress.

A person who experiences a change or crisis usually goes through all or most of the following stages (Westberg, 1971):

1. Shock;

2. Expression of emotion;

3. Depression and loneliness;

4. Physical symptoms of distress;

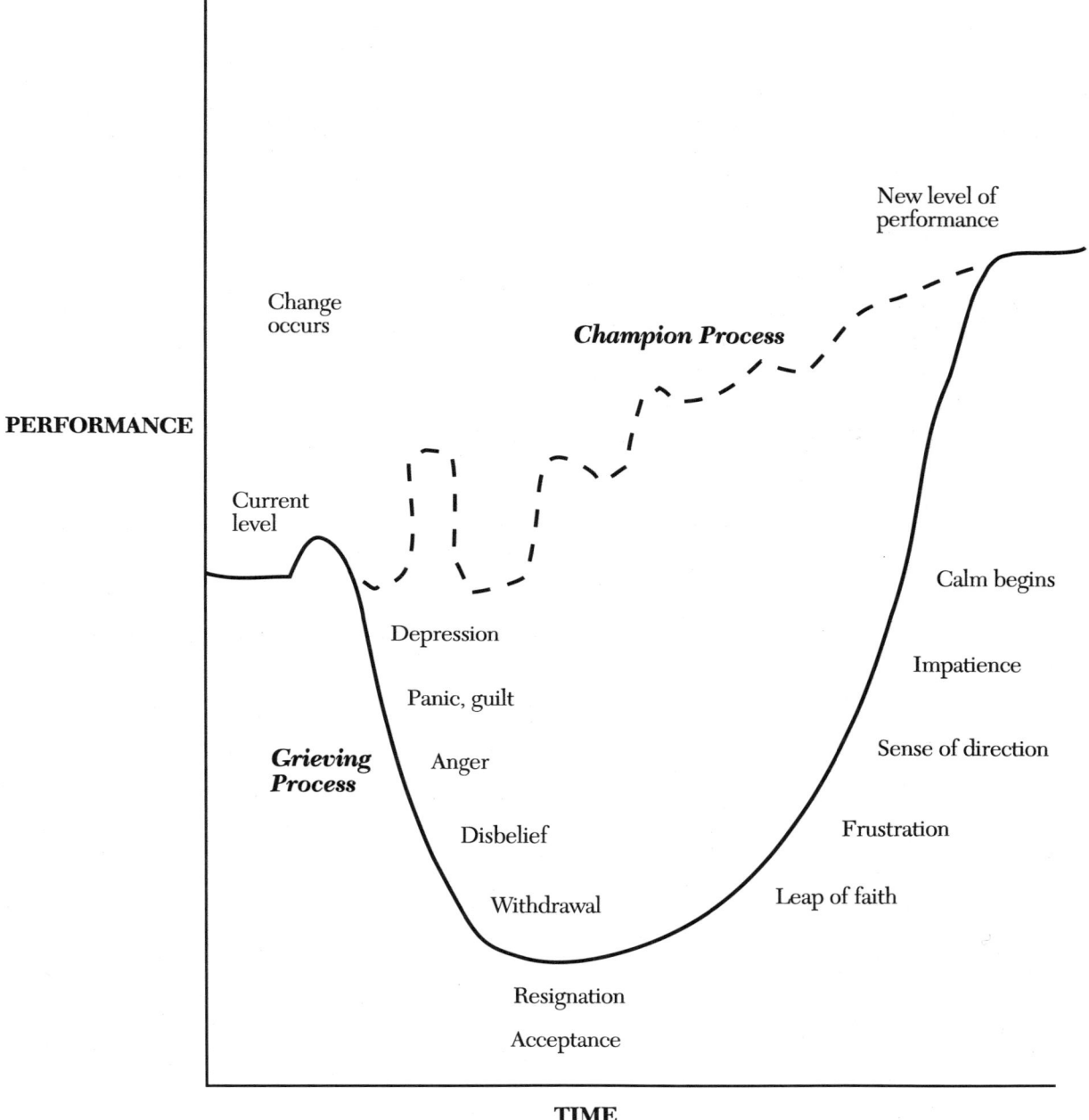

Figure 3. A Model for Understanding Change

5. Panic;

6. Regret and guilt over the fact that something proactive was not done that might have altered the situation or the response to the situation;

7. Anger and resentment;

8. Resistance to returning to the routine;

9. Hope and positive outlook—a leap of faith; and

10. A struggle to affirm reality.

When you are in the early stages, your performance may suffer. But gradually, as you affirm the new reality, your performance will improve. Realize what lies ahead: that you need to work your way through these stages and that doing so is normal. This realization can bring you some comfort.

What To Expect from Others When You Initiate a Change

The chances are that when you want to bring about a change, you will be excited about seeing that change come to fruition. But what about other people who will be affected by the change? Sometimes they appear to "buy in" to a change when you first announce it. Then when they begin to implement the change, they start experiencing the stages of the grieving process. You can help them by assuring them that it is acceptable to have the feelings that accompany that process. Introduce them to the model for understanding change in Figure 3. Suggest that they refer to the model from time to time to check their progress. Encourage them to talk about their feelings.

You can also lessen their grief by making them a part of the change process. Give them a stake in the change so that they become owners and champions. Any change is more acceptable to people when they have the ability to impact how that change is implemented. Listen to their ideas for implementation. Thank them for their contributions and use as many of their ideas as possible.

HOW TO DRAW ON YOUR NETWORK

You can draw on your network for enjoyment, for personal growth, and for help with personal crises.

Using Your Network for Enjoyment

When you accomplish something and you share your excitement with others, you magnify your pleasure. Consequently, when your hobbies produce "masterpieces," share your joy with your friends. Similarly, when you run into temporary roadblocks in creating and want advice on how to do something, ask for help.

Using Your Network for Personal Growth

Close friends in your network can give you feedback about how you are performing, what is being said about you and your staff, how you are perceived, and what potential challenges or opportunities are headed your way. No matter how much the feedback might hurt, thank your colleague for sharing the information. Treat the feedback in confidence and act on it, if action seems appropriate.

If you do not receive this type of feedback spontaneously, approach a reliable, supportive friend and ask for feedback about your performance and related issues. Without feedback, you move through life uncertain of your performance and unclear about how you might improve.

Using Your Network During Crises

When crises strike, many people are embarrassed and want to keep their troubles to themselves. This response is a mistake. Working through a crisis alone is a bleak proposition. Instead, you should contact people near the center of your network when a crisis occurs. Close members of your network want to know such things about you; they want to empathize. Indeed, they find it frustrating to find out two months later that your spouse has died, that you were fired, or whatever. Often they will not be able to do anything except provide support; but you should give them an opportunity to say that they are thinking about you, to express their concern, and to offer help. Let them help you.

Often the challenge lies in figuring out how to tell people about your crisis—how to get the word out. The answer depends to some extent on the type of crisis. If the crisis is a death, most people in your network will want to respond within hours or a day. Even though you are in shock, identify the people you want contacted and then ask your closest friend to pass the message along to those people.

If the crisis is something other than death—being fired, for instance—you may want to take a different approach. First identify the "crisis" people in your network. List a number of them, in case the first ones are not available at the moment. Think of the action that you would like them to take, if any. For example, you may only want to inform them—or you may want someone to discuss the situation over the phone for an hour or so, you may want to visit someone, or you may want someone to come to your home. Realize that your emotions may impede your ability to talk. Consequently, you might find it helpful to write out what you plan to say before you call. Make your comments brief at the beginning of a conversation. Keep trying people until you reach someone who can talk with you; try to contact someone as early as the "shock" stage. Your closest friends will want to help you work through most of the stages of grief that you will experience.

Using Your Network To Get Things Done

You can use your network to get things done at home, at social events, or at work. "To get things done" is defined in the following three ways:

1. To facilitate current activities;
2. To get routine approval; and
3. To make changes.

Facilitating Current Activities

To facilitate many of your current activities, here is what you need:

- To consult with others before acting;

- To receive approval (to be empowered to act, to have the necessary authorization and resources);

- To inform others of your intentions;

- To receive support, services, or information from others (even if they disagree with what you are doing); and

- To act on information supplied by others.

Here is an example of how this process works: André decides that he wants to have a deck added to his house. He *consults* with his wife Annette to see if she agrees; she says that she does. His civil-engineering friends *support* him by helping him design and draw up the plans for the deck. He *receives approval* from the bank for a loan and from the building inspector for the plans. Next he *informs* his neighbors and a number of contractors who might be interested in bidding on the job, and the contractors *support* the idea by submitting bid documents. André *consults* with his friends, former clients of the contractors, and the Better Business Bureau before he *acts* to select a contractor. Suppliers *support* the contractor. When the job has been completed, the contractor *supports* the building inspection and submits a bill to André, *informing* him of the amount owed. Andre *acts* by paying the bill.

In this saga André is responsible for getting the job done. However, to get it done he interacts with many others. Throughout this process the people involved must know what is expected of them and of one another.

Accounting for everyone who facilitates your current activities and determining how each person helps may not be easy. But if you fail to follow through on some of the necessary steps (consulting, receiving support, receiving approval, informing, and acting), the consequences may be serious. For example, you may fail to tell your secretary that you have to dash out of the office for ten minutes to buy a gift for an important client. Maybe you feel that it is silly to bother your secretary with such details. But if your secretary does not know where you are and when you will return, what happens when the company president calls in your absence and urgently needs to speak with you? What can your secretary say? You must give people what they need in order to help you get things done.

———————— ┠┼┨ ————————

✍ Activity 39. Analyzing a Current Task

Consider a task for which you are responsible. The following table has been designed for a work-related task, but if you prefer you may choose a current home activity. Under the appropriate headings in the left column, list the names of people who facilitate this activity. Next to each person's name write the letter that represents that person's role (see the following coding system for roles):

C = Must be *consulted*
I = Must be *informed*
A = Must *approve*
S = Must *support*

Important Note: If too many people have to approve or be consulted, you might never get the job done. If this seems to be the case, consider redesigning the task.

PEOPLE	TASK:	
	What I Expect of Them	*What They Expect of Me*
Customers		
Supervisors		
Peers		

PEOPLE	TASK:	
	What I Expect of Them	*What They Expect of Me*
Service sector (vendors, etc.)		
Subordinates		

You also draw on your network in emergencies or rush situations: when a flyer has to be written, designed, and printed by tomorrow; when a sudden food-services strike means you have to make new arrangements to feed thirty people at a luncheon tomorrow; when a guest speaker tells you twenty minutes before a workshop that he must have a video-playback unit for his presentation. When an emergency occurs, be flexible. Ask for help from the people in your network, but do not be pushy; maintain your relationships with these people.

Getting Routine Approval

In drawing on your network to get approval, you need people to clarify the process for you—to identify who has the power to make the decision and what materials or information (called "deliverables") must be provided so that the decision can be made. In the saga of André's deck, for example, André needed to get approval from the bank for a loan and from the building inspector for the plans. To ensure that these decisions were made, he had to present documentation to the bank manager and technical drawings to the building inspector. In this case he knew what financial documentation the bank manager would need, but he needed help in figuring out what the building inspector would need. His civil-engineering friends were the ones who helped him draw up the technical plans in a form that the building inspector could approve.

Getting approval is like opening a series of gates. In an organization the "gate controllers," the people who grant or refuse approval, have high status in the company. Each of them has control over the activity that leads to one of the gates and can approve resources for the next stage, which in turn leads to another gate.

Figure 4 illustrates the approval process for introducing a new product in a manufacturing organization. Note that each gate has a controller and a specific set of deliverables. Figure 5 is a blank form for identifying decisions, gates, gate controllers, and deliverables; try completing it the next time you want to obtain approval.

Making Changes

Making changes takes a lot of work. It requires the power to mobilize people and the resources to get things done. Kanter (1985) says that 10 percent of the task is the inspiration that gives rise to the idea and 90 percent is the acquisition of power to influence others and to move the idea through the approval procedure.

Implementing change is usually a four-stage process:

Stage 1: Generate the initial idea. You see an opportunity. Because you usually do this alone, Pinchot (1985) calls this the "solo phase."

Stage 2: Modify the idea. You bounce your idea off trusted members of your network to see what they think of it. You are interested in their reactions to the idea, its "political timeliness," and its potential acceptance. You want to identify stakeholders and how the idea might need to be modified to gain their approval. When you present your idea to members of your network, you might want to use a variety of different appeals so that you can determine what evidence and approach would be best when you formally present your idea to stakeholders. Pinchot (1985) calls this the "networking phase," whereas in the context of networking it might be considered as the "inner networking phase."

During this stage you need to develop an understanding of how the system works, who controls what, who influences what, whom to talk to, where the power exists, and how you might gain the support of those in power. Consequently, someone in your trusted inner circle—a power broker or a stakeholder identifier—must have such knowledge.

Stage 3: Gather support. In this stage you use your network for campaigning, lobbying, bargaining, negotiating, and collaborating. Pinchot (1985) calls this the "bootlegging phase" in which you attempt to get others to "buy in" to your idea. This is when you think about the process necessary to get your idea approved, the people who make or influence the key decisions at each gate along the way, and the materials and information ("deliverables") that need to be supplied at each gate.

During this phase you need to have access to power brokers and stakeholder identifiers, to be able to communicate with key people, and to have them understand your view. A power broker not only can identify stakeholders but also can let you know whether they are likely to support your idea, to be against it, to try to sabotage it, or whatever. You need to ensure that you understand how the approval system works—and what the consequences might be if you elect to bypass it.

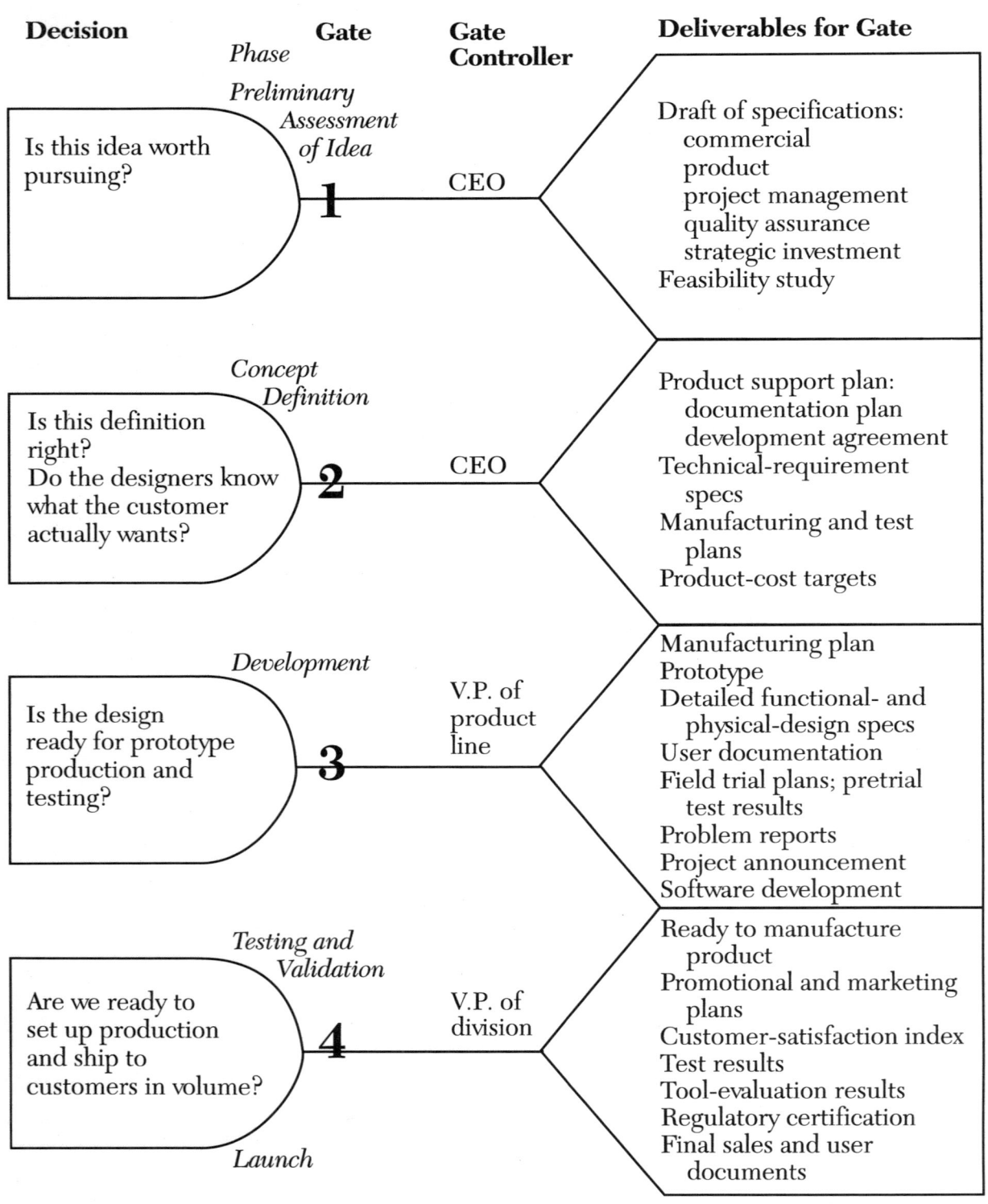

Decision	Phase	Gate	Gate Controller	Deliverables for Gate

Decision   **Gate**   **Gate Controller**   **Deliverables for Gate**

Phase

Preliminary Assessment of Idea

Is this idea worth pursuing?

1   CEO

Draft of specifications:
commercial
product
project management
quality assurance
strategic investment
Feasibility study

Concept Definition

Is this definition right?
Do the designers know what the customer actually wants?

2   CEO

Product support plan:
documentation plan
development agreement
Technical-requirement specs
Manufacturing and test plans
Product-cost targets

Development

Is the design ready for prototype production and testing?

3   V.P. of product line

Manufacturing plan
Prototype
Detailed functional- and physical-design specs
User documentation
Field trial plans; pretrial test results
Problem reports
Project announcement
Software development

Testing and Validation

Are we ready to set up production and ship to customers in volume?

4   V.P. of division

Ready to manufacture product
Promotional and marketing plans
Customer-satisfaction index
Test results
Tool-evaluation results
Regulatory certification
Final sales and user documents

Launch

Figure 4. Approval Process for Introducing a New Product

Decision   **Gate**   **Gate
Controller**   **Deliverables for Gate**

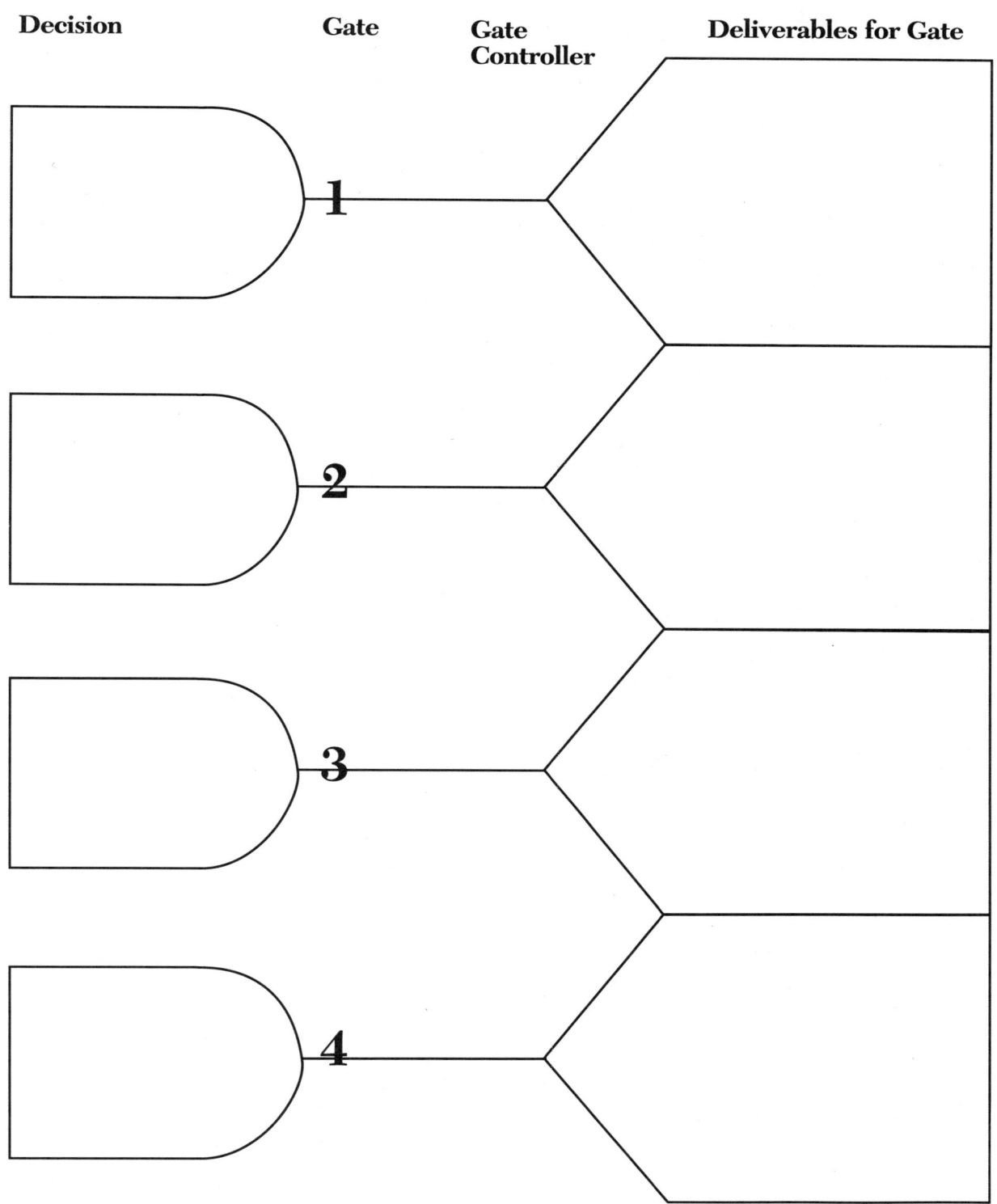

Figure 5. Blank Form for Approval Process

Stage 4: Present the idea and get it approved. In this stage you prepare the necessary documentation, formally present your idea, and nurse it through the approval system. You determine why your idea would be attractive to stakeholders, explore options for getting people to "buy in," and plan your appeal to the various stakeholders. There are five steps involved in this process: (1) developing awareness of organizational procedures, (2) determining the corporate culture and values, (3) identifying the organization's power brokers, (4) identifying the stakeholders who influence the power brokers, and (5) devising strategies for approaching people to get support.

Step 1. Developing awareness of organizational procedures. You need to be aware of the process used for making decisions. Go to people in your network for information about who grants approval (who the gate controllers are) and what deliverables are expected. Various members of your network will be able to give you valuable information about what motivates the gate controllers: Are they concerned about the environment? the bottom line? a sense of teamwork among employees? the image of the company in the community?

Step 2. Determining the corporate culture and values. The "deliverables" that must be provided to facilitate decision making may be stated or unstated, but they are always based on the organization's value system. Values are something that the company takes pride in; they affect all decisions. Some companies have explicit statements of values that are distributed to all employees, but many do not. If your organization does not have an explicit values statement, you have to look to other sources. Check the organizational credo, slogan, or vision statement. (The mission statement, however, will probably not be helpful.)

Organizational decisions are excellent indicators of values. Examine recent decisions and any rationales that were shared with employees; if no rationales were shared, ask your supervisor and peers to help you determine those rationales. Also ask your peers, your supervisor, and your subordinates to give you their assessments of the values that drive the organization; their opinions can be very helpful.

Another way to determine organizational values is to take an instrument or questionnaire that pinpoints values—and to ask peers to do the same and to share their results with you. For example, Francis and Woodcock (1990) suggest that organizations focus on four basically different values to which they attribute success: (1) the quality of *management,* (2) the quality of *relationships* among employees, (3) the attitude toward the *external environment,* and (4) the skill in doing the *task.* They offer the "Organizational Values Questionnaire," an instrument that you can take to help you assess which is the dominant culture in your organization. Similarly, there are other instruments that you can obtain and complete that will provide you with an understanding of your organization's values and culture (see, for example, Harrison and Stokes, 1992).

Once you have determined what the organizational values are, you will be able to evaluate your chances for success in making the change you want. You will also be able to offer an appropriate rationale for the change that will garner the support you need. For example, if it is important to your company to have employees feel as if they are part of a family, then you know that any change you propose will be judged on how well it supports this concept.

Step 3. Identifying the organization's power brokers. Although it may seem apparent who your organization's power brokers are, sometimes appearances are deceiving. The authors recommend that you test your intuition in this matter against two criteria: (1) the corporate-culture criterion and (2) the Whetten and Cameron (1984) power criterion.

The corporate-culture criterion is that the person in question must *support and demonstrate the corporate values.* He or she must be a walking example of the organizational culture. In addition, Whetten and Cameron (1984) suggest that to be a power broker, a person must possess power because of his or her position and personal attributes. The person's position must be central and *critical* to work flow; *flexible,* involving a lot of discretion; *visible,* necessitating interaction with many other people; and *relevant* to the tasks and priorities of the organization. A power broker's personal attributes must include *expertise, a willingness to expend extra effort,* and *strong interpersonal skills.* What is interesting about these criteria is that they sum up most of the characteristics of successful networking or networkers.

✍ Activity 40. Identifying Power Brokers

For your organization or community, list people that you believe to be power brokers. Then apply the above criteria to determine whether these people are, in fact, power brokers. If someone is not a power broker, note which skill or criterion is missing.

Step 4. Identifying the stakeholders who influence the power brokers. To be able to make a change, you need to influence the power brokers and minimize resistance to the change. Stakeholders—those who might be affected by the change—can either help you convince the power brokers that the change is worthwhile or defeat your idea. Consequently, you must identify all stakeholders. Then you must determine each stakeholder's stance on the change (in favor of it, neutral, or against it—and to what degree), the level of trust between you and each stakeholder, and each stakeholder's position in the organizational hierarchy relative to your own (supervisor, peer, or subordinate).

For any change that you would like to make, you will encounter stakeholders with a variety of stances. Focus your efforts on the critical few—those whose support you must have. You do not have to convince everyone to be in favor of the change; you just have to ensure that the critical few support you and that the other stakeholders will allow you to proceed without sabotaging the change after it has been approved.

━━━━━━━━━━━━━━━ ┼┼┼ ━━━━━━━━━━━━━━━

✍ Activity 41. Assessing Stakeholders

Think of a change that you would like to implement in your organization. Identify the stakeholders by name or initials. Then put check marks in the appropriate columns to indicate each stakeholder's stance (In Favor, Neutral, or Against), the level of trust in your relationship with each stakeholder (High, Unknown, or Low), and each stakeholder's position in the organizational hierarchy relative to your own (Supervisor, Peer, or Subordinate).

If you have trouble with this task, list the names of stakeholder identifiers who might help you. (A stakeholder identifier is someone who is aware of the corporate culture and the concerns and turfs of most employees. For more information, see "Setting Goals for Networks and Networking" in Chapter 2.)

Stakeholders	Stance			Trust			Position		
	In Favor	*Neutral*	*Against*	*High*	*Un-known*	*Low*	*Super-visor*	*Peer*	*Subor-dinate*
Those whose support is essential:									

Stakeholders	Stance			Trust			Position		
	In Favor	Neutral	Against	High	Un-known	Low	Super-visor	Peer	Subor-dinate
Those whose support would be helpful:									

Step 5. Devising strategies for approaching people to get support. Block (1987), Beckhard and Harris (1987), and Kanter (1985) offer suggestions.

Block (1987) outlines steps for one-on-one discussions with five different classes of stakeholders:

High-trust person who is in favor of the change

1. Affirm agreement about the change.
2. Reaffirm the quality of the relationship; let the other person know how you feel about him or her. Comments like "I trust what you are telling me" are appropriate.
3. Acknowledge your doubts and vulnerability with respect to your goals.
4. Ask for support and advice.

High-trust person who is against the change

1. Reaffirm the quality of your relationship and the trust in that relationship.
2. State your position about the change.
3. State in a neutral way what you think the other person's position is.
4. Engage in some type of problem solving, openly exploring differences.

Low-trust person who is in favor of the change

1. Reaffirm the agreement about the change.

2. Acknowledge that caution exists.

3. Be clear as to what you want from the other person in terms of working together.

4. Ask the other person what he or she wants from you.

5. Try to reach agreement regarding how the two of you are going to work together.

Low-trust person who is against the change

1. State your view of the change.

2. State in a neutral way your best understanding of the other person's position.

3. Identify your own contribution to the problem of disagreement. Explain what actions you have taken to try to get the other person's support of the change.

4. State that you respect the other person's point of view. Acknowledge that the two of you agree to disagree. End the meeting with no plans and no demands. (Your purpose is to negotiate trust.)

Low-trust person who is neutral about the change

1. State your position on the change; explain your purpose, mission, and vision.

2. Ask where the other person stands.

3. Apply gentle pressure.

4. Encourage the other person to think about the change and to let you know what it would take for him or her to give you support.

Beckhard and Harris (1987) offer suggestions as follows:

Find the problem

Unfreeze the opposition; make it neutral. Meet with stakeholders as a group to clarify issues. Listen to one another. Allow no action, no taking of minutes. Use a minimum of group structure. Seek to understand everyone's position and to identify areas of agreement and disagreement.

Intervene with education

Hold educational seminars. Consider using the services of an outside expert; such people can have great impact. Describe the change process and how to cope with the accompanying frustration and so on.

Negotiate/manage the resistance

Identify the extent and the source. Personally visit with people who oppose the change.

Role model

Practice what you preach.

Force

Change the situation, the reward system, and/or the people on the team. Force resistors to leave.

Kanter (1985) suggests first clearing the change with your immediate supervisor and then gathering support from peers and people below you in the organizational hierarchy. She recommends one-on-one meetings with each person on his or her turf. During each meeting you should act as though the other person is critical to the success of the change. After you have completed these meetings, consult those high in the hierarchy, presenting a very specific description of the proposed change.

It is a good idea to practice strategies by role playing real situations in which you try to win the support of stakeholders. Choose two friends to work with you, making sure that they agree not to disclose the content of the role plays to others. Carefully explain the situation to them and what you are trying to accomplish. One friend will play the role of a specific stakeholder. Define the stakeholder's role, clarifying the details of his or her stance and the level of trust in your relationship with that stakeholder. The other friend will observe your interchange with the stakeholder, making notes about the following aspects of the conversation:

Your listening and your responses. Are you attending to the other person (by making eye contact, for example)? Are you following the conversation (by restating the other person's position when appropriate, for example)? Are you being assertive? Are you demonstrating empathy? Are your responses appropriate for the context and content of the conversation?

The effectiveness of your strategy in terms of achieving "buy-in." Have you clearly stated your stance? Has your stance been understood by the other person? Is your strategy appropriate for the person and the situation? Have you monitored the progress of the conversation and altered your strategy if necessary?

The effectiveness of your strategy in terms of building trust. Have you promoted trust in an appropriate way? Have you demonstrated honesty and openness? Have you been careful not to push for more trust than you are willing to give in return?

After the conversation the three of you discuss the experience. The observer summarizes the content of his or her notes, highlighting five strengths that you demonstrated and suggesting two areas to work on. Then you and the stakeholder share thoughts and feelings. If you conduct another role play, the observer and stakeholder should switch roles so that you can receive the benefit of different perspectives.

Regardless of which strategies you choose in actual attempts to gain support, focus on using your network. Because it is important to give people time to adjust, you need to provide them with advance notice of the need or opportunity that the change addresses, the options being considered, and the ultimate decision. As much as possible, encourage them to discuss the change. If those who will be affected are allowed to offer input, there is greater likelihood that they will own the change and champion it. Also, if people consider and address potential problems that may be encountered during implementation, the chances are that implementation will go more smoothly. Remember, too, that while people are trying to implement the change, you must support them through the grieving process.

SUMMARY

Your network is a powerful resource for making things happen. If you are to draw on it effectively, you must be positive and ask for help and you must understand and accept the nature of change. There are many ways to draw on your network: for enjoyment, for personal growth, during crises, and to get things done. You depend on various kinds of assistance from many people to accomplish things in your life. For instance, others facilitate your current activities and help you to get routine approval.

You can also use your network to make changes. When you do, you need to remember that change is difficult and generally has a negative effect on performance as people try to adjust to it. You need to support yourself and others during the grieving process that often accompanies change. To make changes in an organizational setting, you must determine your organization's culture and values, identify the organization's power brokers, identify the stakeholders who influence the power brokers, and then devise strategies for approaching people to get their support for the changes you propose.

———————————— ┼┼┼ ————————————

✍ Activity 42. Discoveries from Chapter 8

Write what you have discovered as a result of reading and working through this chapter. Add how you might apply the discovered ideas in your daily living.

Discovery	Application
Ask assertively	

Discovery	Application
Change:	
Grieving process	
Champion process	
Networking for enjoyment	
Networking for personal growth	
Networking during crises	
Networking to get things done	
Facilitating current activities	
Getting approval	
Making changes:	
Generate the idea	

Discovery	Application
Modify the idea	
Gather support	
Present the idea and get it approved	
Organizational procedures: Gate controllers	
Corporate culture and values	
Power brokers	
Stakeholders	
Strategies for getting support	
Other	

✍ *Activity 43. Action Plan for the Coming Week*

Identify one area from the discoveries activity that you want to work on. Create an action plan for the coming week for improving in that area. Use the following space to make notes about your plan and your progress.

9

Facilitating Networking in an Organization

OVERVIEW OF THIS CHAPTER

An organization can either help or hinder you in your networking efforts. This chapter offers suggestions for making your organization's environment more conducive to networking.

IDEAS FOR FACILITATING NETWORKING

Here are some ideas for facilitating networking in an organization (DeMarco, Rosenfeld, & Varian, 1989; Kanter, 1985). If you are in a managerial position, discuss these ideas with your fellow managers and work toward their implementation. If you are in a nonmanagerial position, discuss them with your supervisor and ask that he or she bring them up at a managers' meeting.

1. Encourage frequent mobility. Changing positions or responsibilities every one and one-half to two years facilitates networking.

2. Offer job security or "permanent employment" so that the time that people invest in internal networking will pay off.

3. Ensure that the criteria used for performance reviews recognize, reward, and encourage networking. Abbott (1988) points out that the skills of networkers ("gatekeepers" in his terminology) are rarely recognized or rewarded and that networkers tend to be the first to go during cutbacks. This situation needs to change. Rewards need not be monetary; recognition can do much to facilitate networking.

4. Use teams or task forces frequently to address issues. They provide excellent opportunities for networking. The increased use of teams may mean that people will need training in teamwork and team building.

5. Create an environment of nonrestrictive protocols and "unprotected turf" so that people can cross boundaries with ease and have local access to resources.

6. Identify superior networkers and make them responsible for facilitating the change process. Typically such people would rather apply their creative efforts to changing the constraints of the system rather than work within those constraints. Amoco and Union Carbide have set up internal "offices of innovation" to which people can bring their ideas. The director of such an office then facilitates the necessary networking to assess and perhaps implement those ideas.

In addition, as discussed in Chapter 6, people should be provided with "naked time" (M. Spears, personal communication, 1990)—time to observe how decisions are made, to learn how things get done. They also should be made aware of corporate values, structure, procedures, power brokers, and stakeholder identifiers. Finally, they should be given specific information about what constitutes networking on behalf of the organization; appropriate amounts should be allocated in the budget for such networking.

SUMMARY

A variety of practical changes to an organization's environment can make networking easier: encouraging job mobility, offering job security, including networking in performance reviews (recognizing and rewarding networking), using teams or task forces, minimizing the amount of "protected turf," identifying superior networkers and using them as change agents, providing people with "naked time," making people aware of information they need to network effectively, telling people what constitutes networking for the organization, and allocating money for organizational networking.

---- ┼┼┼ ----

✍ Activity 44. Facilitating Organizational Networking

For your current situation and the tasks and projects over which you have control, identify actions that you could take to improve networking in your organization.

1. Encourage job mobility

2. Recognize and reward networking

3. Use teams and task forces

4. Promote unprotected turf

5. Organize a networking function, newsletter, etc.

6. Allow "naked time"

7. Budget for networking

✍ Activity 45. Discoveries from Chapter 9

Write what you have discovered as a result of reading and working through this chapter. Add how you might apply the discovered ideas in your daily living.

Discovery	Application
Environment has impact on networking effectiveness	
Allow employees "naked time"	
Encourage mobility, job security	
Include networking in performance reviews; reward	
Use teams; train in teamwork and team building	
Minimize "protected turf"	
Use superior networkers as change agents	

Discovery

Allocate money for networking

Other

—————————— ╫╫ ——————————

✍ Activity 46. Action Plan for the Coming Week

Identify one area from the discoveries activity that you want to work on. Create an action plan for the coming week for improving in that area. Use the following space to make notes about your plan and your progress.

Application

10

Review and Action Planning

OVERVIEW OF THIS CHAPTER

This chapter offers you a chance to reflect on your experiences in reading and working through this book. It also gives you an opportunity to do some action planning.

You should congratulate yourself on the good work you have done. You have identified your current network; reflected on the principles of networking; and considered how to create, nurture, and expand your network. Now you can put your ideas to work by developing a pattern of networking in your life. Anne Boe (1986) recommends that networking become a lifestyle. Careful action planning is the best way to make that happen.

REVIEW OF CHAPTERS 1 THROUGH 9

Before you develop your action plan, review the activities in each of the preceding chapters. Then read and mentally answer the questions listed under "Questions to Consider."

Chapter 1: Networks and Networking

Activities

1. Bridging (p. 3)
2. Current Awareness and Skill (p. 8)
3. Discoveries from Chapter 1 (p. 9)
4. Action Plan for the Coming Week (p. 10)

Questions to Consider

- Am I familiar with the characteristics of effective networking so that I can apply them in my own networking efforts?

- Do I know how to use bridging to obtain access to someone I do not know?

Chapter 2: Setting Goals for Networks and Networking

Activities

5. Goal Setting (p. 12)
6. Networking Table (p. 15)
7. Diagram of Your Network (p. 16)
8. Assessing Your Current Network (p. 19)
9. Discoveries from Chapter 2 (p. 21)
10. Action Plan for the Next Month (p. 22)

Questions to Consider

- Does my network help me to achieve my goals?

- When I set a goal, do I write it down, include milestones and criteria, and make sure that it is achievable and consistent with my lifetime objectives?

- Does my network include at least four people, from a variety of sources, whom I can count on during a crisis; at least three people with whom I can share activities that I enjoy; at least twelve people who can help me achieve my goals and get things done; at least as many people below me in the organizational hierarchy as above me; at least one organizational power broker; and at least one stakeholder identifier?

Chapter 3: Skills for Effective Networking

Activities

11. Practicing Positive Self-Talk (p. 26)
12. Assessing Interpersonal Skills (p. 30)
13. Designing Appropriate Responses (p. 32)
14. Discoveries from Chapter 3 (p. 35)
15. Action Plan for the Coming Week (p. 36)

Questions to Consider

- Do I have a plan for developing my self-awareness?

- Do I show empathy, understanding, and genuineness in my interactions with others? Do I understand and accept the viewpoints of others, even when I disagree with them?

- Do I make my thoughts and feelings known and promote recognition of myself as an individual?

- Do I honor the fundamental human rights?

- Do I follow the guidelines for "interpersonal Shangri-la"?

Chapter 4: Principles of Effective Networking

Activities

Questions to Consider

- Do I do what I say I will do?

- Do I meet or exceed the expectations of others?

- Do I do my work on time and within budget?

- Do I do my work right the first time?

- Do I follow through?

- Do I anticipate problems and develop contingency plans?

- Do I set and prioritize goals?

- Am I nurturing and supportive to others?

- Does my network include many different kinds of people with diverse interests and backgrounds?

- Have I established visibility at work, among my former classmates, within my profession, and in my neighborhood?

- Have I established ways to learn about the unique characteristics of other people?

• Do I organize information about others in a way that facilitates networking?

Chapter 5: Nurturing Your Network

Activities

Questions to Consider

• Am I available, reliable, and generous in sharing my experience and ideas with others and in providing them with support?

• Am I trustworthy and discreet?

• Do I listen carefully to others?

• In what ways do I promote the recognition of others?

• What personal touches do I use to keep my network alive?

• In what ways do I support people during crises?

• What plans do I have for retrieving people who have drifted from me?

Chapter 6: Expanding Your Network

Activities

Questions to Consider

• In what ways do I take the initiative to bring necessary people into my network?

• Do I have a mentor? If not, what are my plans for inviting someone to be my mentor?

- Am I effective in being a mentor to others? Do I listen and then willingly offer information and give guidance?

- Do I systematically volunteer to work on special projects or to serve on special committees?

- Do I take advantage of opportunities to chat informally in various settings?

- Do I have business cards that are classy and appealing? Do I exchange them with others?

- Do I occasionally change my routine so that I can meet people?

- When I join a new organization, do I allow myself "naked time" to listen and to observe how decisions are made? How much "naked time" do I allow my subordinates when they join my department or division?

Chapter 7: Coping with the "Down" Side of Networking

Activities

36. Saying "No" (p. 75)
37. Discoveries from Chapter 7 (p. 77)
38. Action Plan for the Coming Week (p. 78)

Questions to Consider

- How do you react when you encounter difficult behaviors in others?

- How effectively do you manage your commitments? Are you able to say "no" comfortably?

- Are you willing to take calculated risks?

- Are you patient in your networking efforts, realizing that it takes time to develop trust and warmth in relationships? Do you celebrate your progress?

- Before you invite people into your network, do you make sure that you are willing and able to give at least as much as you take?

- Have you established a policy for handling money issues related to networking?

Chapter 8: Drawing on Your Network

Activities

39. Analyzing a Current Task (p. 85)
40. Identifying Power Brokers (p. 91)
41. Assessing Stakeholders (p. 92)

42. Discoveries from Chapter 8 (p. 96)

43. Action Plan for the Coming Week (p. 99)

Questions to Consider

- Do I use an assertive and mannerly approach in asking for what I need?

- Do I acknowledge that change is difficult and that performance may suffer in the early stages?

- Do I support and encourage others as they go through the change process? Do I listen to their ideas for implementation, thank them for their ideas, and incorporate as many of those ideas as possible?

- Do I share my accomplishments with others? Do I ask them for help and advice when I run into roadblocks?

- Do I ask for feedback that would help me achieve personal growth?

- Do I call on my network during crises?

- Do I know what various people need in order to help me get things done? Do I meet their needs?

- Can I identify the organizational gate controllers that I must deal with? Do I know what must be delivered to each controller?

- Do I understand the process for making organizational changes? Can I identify power brokers and stakeholder identifiers?

- Do I know how to approach people to obtain their support for my ideas?

Chapter 9: Facilitating Networking in an Organization

Activities

44. Facilitating Organizational Networking (p. 102)

45. Discoveries from Chapter 9 (p. 104)

46. Action Plan for the Coming Week (p. 105)

Questions to Consider

- How would you assess your organization's current approach to networking? What specific programs or policies exist?

- What can you do to encourage job mobility, recognize and reward networking, encourage the use of teams and task forces, promote unprotected turf, organize a networking function or newsletter, allow "naked time," and budget for networking?

Activity 47. Reassessing Awareness and Skill

How *aware* are you of your current network and of what you do when you are networking? On the following continuum, circle the number that describes your level of awareness.

0   1   2   3   4   5   6   7   8   9   10

Unaware;   Somewhat   Very aware;
I just   aware   I can describe
do it   details

How *skilled* are you at networking? On the following continuum, circle the number that describes your level of skill.

0   1   2   3   4   5   6   7   8   9   10

Poor   Fair   Good   Very good   Excellent

This assessment also appeared in Chapter 1 as Activity 2 (p. 8). Review your previous assessment of your awareness and skill and compare it with this one. What do the results tell you?

ACTION PLAN

Now that you have reviewed the content of Chapters 1 through 9, you are ready to construct your action plan.

✍ Activity 48. Creating an Action Plan

Most of the activities in this book dealt with tasks to be completed over a period of a week or so. Now is the time for long-range planning. Create a networking goal for yourself, determine milestones, establish criteria, and figure out what resources and support are necessary. In the section labeled "Resources/support that I need," include the names, addresses, and phone and fax numbers of people whose help you will need. Set dates not only for reaching your goal and milestones but also for reviewing your progress along the way. After you have written your goal, make sure that it is achievable and consistent with your lifetime objectives; if it is not, rework it until it is.

If you need to review the process of setting goals, refer to Chapter 2.

Goal: **Criteria**

Resources/support that I need (including names, addresses, etc.):

Completion date:_____

Milestone: **Criteria**

Resources/support that I need (including names, addresses, etc.):

Completion date:_____

Milestone: **Criteria**

Resources/support that I need (including names, addresses, etc.):

Completion date:_____

Milestone: **Criteria**

Resources/support that I need (including names, addresses, etc.):

Completion date:_____

Dates on which I will review my progress:

_____

_____

_____

_____

_____

_____

Remember to share your vision with your support people and draw on their support as you implement your action plan. Morrison et al. (1987) emphasize that to help others help you, you must let them know about your goals. The more specifically you are able to describe your plans, the easier it is for others to help. Remember, too, that the route to a goal involves failures and setbacks as well as successes. Keep the overall goal in sight, learn from your disappointments, and rejoice at your achievements.

SUMMARY

This chapter offered you a chance to review the content of Chapters 1 through 9 and to devise an action plan for achieving a networking goal. It also emphasized the importance of developing a pattern of networking in your life. If you turn networking into a lifestyle, you will reap the benefits of an enriched life and an enhanced ability to get things done.

References

Abbott, M. (1988, November 14-15). *Management of technology: Fundamentals*. Workshop conducted for Ontario Hydro, Toronto, Ontario, Canada.

Arnold, J.D. (1978). *Make up your mind!* New York: AMACOM.

Beckhard, R., & Harris, R.T. (1987). *Organizational transitions: Managing complex change* (2nd ed.). Reading, MA: Addison-Wesley.

Black, G. (1982, October 4). The new job: Settling in gracefully. *Chemical Engineering,* pp. 129-132.

Bliss, E.C. (1976). *Getting things done.* New York: Bantam.

Block, P. (1987). *The empowered manager: Positive political skills at work.* San Francisco: Jossey-Bass.

Boe, A. (1986, October 27). Networking: New contact sport for managers. *Chemical Engineering,* pp. 145-146.

Boe, A., & Youngs, B.B. (1989). *Is your "net" working?* New York: John Wiley.

Bolton, R. (1979). *People skills: How to assert yourself, listen to others and resolve conflicts.* New York: Simon & Schuster.

Brothers, J. (1978). *How to get whatever you want out of life.* New York: Ballantine.

Bushardt, S.C., & Fowler, A.R., Jr. (1989). The art of feedback: Providing constructive information. In J.W. Pfeiffer (Ed.), *The 1989 annual: Developing human resources* (pp. 9-16). San Diego, CA: Pfeiffer & Company.

Cava, R. (1988). *Escaping the pink collar ghetto.* Toronto, Ontario, Canada: Key Porter Books.

Cawood, D. (1988). *Assertiveness for managers* (2nd ed.). Toronto, Ontario, Canada: Self Counsel Press.

Covey, S.R. (1989). *The seven habits of highly effective people: Restoring the character ethic.* New York: Simon & Schuster.

DeMarco, D.A., Rosenfeld, R., & Varian, E.S., Jr. (1989, November). *Innovation in the chemical industry.* Session at the American Institute of Chemical Engineers' Annual Meeting, San Francisco.

Francis, D., & Woodcock, M. (1990). *Unblocking organizational values.* San Diego, CA: Pfeiffer & Company.

Gotlieb, S. (1990). *Washington rollercoaster.* New York: Doubleday.

Harrison, R., & Stokes, H. (1992). *Diagnosing organizational culture.* San Diego, CA: Pfeiffer & Company.

Johnson, D.W. (1986). *Reaching out* (3rd ed.) Englewood Cliffs, NJ: Prentice-Hall.

Kanter, R.M. (1985). *The change masters: Innovation and productivity in the American corporation.* New York: Simon & Schuster.

Kassorla, I.C. (1984). *Go for it!* New York: Dell.

Kelley, C. (1979). *Assertion training: A facilitator's guide.* San Diego, CA: Pfeiffer & Co.

Kepner, C.H., & Tregoe, B.B. (1965). *The rational manager.* New York: McGraw-Hill.

Kirkpatrick, D.L. (1985). *How to manage change effectively.* San Francisco: Jossey-Bass.

Lakein, A. (1973). *How to get control of your time and your life.* New York: Signet.

Locke, E.A., Shaw, K.N., Saari, L.M., & Latham, G.P. (1981). Goal setting and task performance: 1969-1980. *Psychological Bulletin, 90*(1), 125-152.

MacKenzie, R.A. (1975). *The time trap: How to get more done in less time.* New York: McGraw-Hill.

Meichenbaum, D. (1983). *Coping with stress.* New York: John Wiley.

Morrison, A.N., White, R.P., & van Velson, E. (1987). *Breaking the glass ceiling.* Reading, MA: Addison-Wesley.

Peale, N.V. (1969). *The power of positive thinking.* New York: Fawcett World Library.

Pinchot, G., III. (1985). *Intrapreneuring.* New York: Harper & Row.

Rhode, H. (1989). *Assertiveness training for professionals.* Videotape produced by Career-Trak, Boulder, CO.

Rusk, T., & Rusk, N. (1988). *Mind traps: Change your mind, change your life.* Los Angeles: Price Stern Sloan.

Schiavoni, M.R. (1984, February 6). Assimilating the new manager. *Chemical Engineering,* pp. 117-120.

Taylor, H.L. (1981). *Making time work for you.* Toronto, Ontario, Canada: General Publishing Co.

Weldon, J. (1982). *Jet pilots don't use rear view mirrors.* Business seminar prepared for American Airlines by Joel H. Weldon & Associates, Inc., 7975 N. Hayden Rd., Suite D-147, Scottsdale, AZ 85258.

Westberg, G.E. (1971). *Good grief.* Philadelphia, PA: Fortress Press.

Whetten, D.A., & Cameron, K.S. (1984). *Developing management skills.* Glenview, IL: Scott, Foresman.

Ziglar, Z. (1986). *Top performance.* New York: Berkeley Books.

About the Authors

Donald R. Woods, Ph.D., is a professor of chemical engineering at McMaster University in Hamilton, Ontario, Canada, where he also serves as the director of the Engineering and Management Program. He belongs to the Canadian Society of Chemical Engineers, the American Institute of Chemical Engineers, and the Association of Professional Engineers of Ontario. He has been named a 3M Fellow for being Outstanding Canadian Educator, and McMaster University's Faculty of Engineering has awarded him a Citation for Innovations in Education.

For the past twenty years Don has developed workshop and self-study materials in the areas of problem solving and interpersonal-skills development. More recently he has concentrated on networking. His materials have been used in industries, universities, and businesses in North America, Australia, and the People's Republic of China.

Shirley D. Ormerod is a program assistant in McMaster University's Engineering and Management Program. As an administrator and counselor, she facilitates the day-to-day operations of this program. She also is responsible for instructing students on effective job-search strategies as well as oral- and written-communication skills. In 1988 she developed the Summer Work Experience Program for students in Engineering and Management, and since that time she has served as both coordinator and instructor of this program.

Like her coauthor, Shirley is an avid networker. Repeated inquiries about how she became so accomplished at networking led her to develop the material in this book. She has run workshops not only on networking but also on communication skills, problem solving, and effective job-search strategies.

|||

Developmental Editing: ***Carol Nolde***

Cover Design: ***Paul Bond***

Interior Design and Page Composition: ***Judy Whalen***

This book was edited and formatted using 486 PC platforms with 8MB RAM and high-resolution, dual-page monitors. The copy was produced using Word-Perfect software; pages were composed with Ventura Publisher software. The text is set in New Caledonia, and the heads are set in Britannic. Proof copies were printed on a 400-dpi laser printer and final camera-ready output on a 1200-dpi laser imagesetter by Pfeiffer & Company.